ERROR

(On Our Predicament
When Things Go Wrong)

ERROR

(On Our Predicament When Things Go Wrong)

NICHOLAS RESCHER

University of Pittsburgh Press

Published by the University of Pittsburgh Press, Pittsburgh, PA 15260

Copyright © 2007, University of Pittsburgh Press

Manufactured in the United States of America

Printed on acid-free paper

10 9 8 7 6 5 4 3 2 1

Library of Congress Cataloging-in-Publication Data

Rescher, Nicholas.
    Error : on our predicament when things go wrong / Nicholas Rescher.
        p.   cm.
    Includes bibliographical references and index.
    ISBN 0-8229-4327-1 (cloth : alk. paper)
    1. Error.   I. Title.
    BD171.R47 2007
    121'.6—dc22   2006026043

To Robert Almeder
in cordial friendship

CONTENTS

PREFACE

In their single-track concern for the knowledge of truth recent episte-
mologists have neglected to address the dark side of the issue: our all
too common belief in falsehoods. Preoccupied with what goes well
in matters of cognition, they have tended to overlook the surely no
less prominent region of the things that go wrong.

This has not always been so. Error has long been a prominent topic
in philosophy, and as late as the 1960s Macmillan's seven-volume *Encyclopedia of Philosophy* had a long article on the subject. Puzzlingly,
however, it has been rather neglected in recent years, and for some
incomprehensible reason has nowadays pretty much vanished from
the Anglo-American scene. For whatever reason, the topic is absent
from the index of Oxford University Press's *Handbook of Philosophy*
(2002), from Routledge's *An Encyclopedia of Philosophy* (1988), from
Cambridge University Press's *Directory of Philosophy* (1990), and from
Blackwell's *Companion to Epistemology* (1992). It would seem that this
topic had pretty much dropped out of sight as a topic of philosophical
concern toward the end of the twentieth century. So, while there is
no reason to think that the role of error in human affairs has become

any less significant, its role as an object of philosophical concern has decidedly diminished in recent years. The present book, however, is written in the firm conviction that the older tradition has it right and that the topic of error decidedly merits the attention of philosophers.

Conceived in Pittsburgh in the spring of 2005, the book was drafted in Oxford during that summer and subsequently polished in Pittsburgh. I am very grateful to Alan Musgrave, as well as an anonymous publisher's reader, for constructive criticism, and to Estelle Burris for her able help in putting my manuscript into publishable form.

Pittsburgh, PA
December 2005

ERROR

(On Our Predicament
When Things Go Wrong)

1

The Ways of Error

BASICS

One can in principle err about pretty well anything. The three prime spheres of human concern are belief, behavior, and evaluation, which correlate with matters of fact, action, and value. And one can manage to err in all three settings. There are three main categories of error: *Cognitive* error arises from failures in the attainment of correct beliefs; *practical* error arises from failures in relation to the objectives of action; *axiological* error appertains to mistakes in regard to evaluation. Where there is cognitive error, one inclines to question the quality of the agent's intellect; with practical error, the quality of the agent's competence; and with evaluative error, the quality of the agent's judgment, if not character. However, in an intelligent being, whose actions issue from beliefs through the mediation of judgments, the three kinds of error are closely interrelated. Accordingly, the children's jingle "Sticks and stones may break my bones but names will never hurt me" does not get matters right. For words are the vehicle of our thought; and where our thoughts go wrong, so will the actions that we inevitably guide by them; and wrong actions can, of course, prove to be very hurtful indeed.

Error is commonplace in human affairs because *Homo sapiens* are limited creatures whose needs and wants outrun their available capabilities. A liability to error is thus inherent in the very nature of our situation as beings of limited experience in a world of endless complexity. And specifically cognitive error roots in our human need to resolve issues of thought and action in conditions of imperfect information. Such error is common, because for every issue of decision, be it cognitive or practical, there is a multitude of conflicting responses of very different degrees of merit, and to our finite and fallible minds many of those goats seems altogether sheeplike to us—save on the closest and most painstaking inspection.

In the end, error is inevitable for us humans because, being intelligent creatures who act on the guidance of our beliefs, we base our decisions and actions on information, and even the best information available at the time is as often as not inaccurate. Our beliefs are based on our experience, and our experience is an incomplete and imperfect indicator for the generality of things. In shaping our beliefs we conform them to the *available* information, and this inevitably leads us to oversimplify, to generalize, where what is actually needed is qualification and complexification.

Error is a matter of getting things wrong. When intending to do X, one does Y instead—such as typing *casual* instead of *causal*—one makes an error. Committing an error accordingly involves a counterproductive act, the doing or omission of something one would fain alter. For error is a matter of actions—of *wrongdoing* in the case of practical error and *wrongthinking* (if only such a term were available) in the case of cognitive errors. Errors do not simply happen by themselves; they do not just occur but are made. Thus in his *Rhetoric* Aristotle characterizes a mistake *(hamartêma)* as a mishap that cannot be altogether surprising. For we human agents are prone to error, and mistakes (unlike misfortunes, *atuchêma*) are always the result of human agency. We say, "John *made* an error," and not, "An error happened to John." A being unable to act voluntarily can indeed do things that are counterproductive to its interests and indeed can even act self-destructively; but it does not commit errors, save when we speak figuratively. Inert devices—machines and instruments—do not commit errors; they malfunction, that is, fail to work as intended by their deviser. But they do not err when this occurs.

Errors generally arise in relation to aims and purposes. They require intention—at least implicitly regarding the sorts of purposes that people *should* have. Error is a fundamental purposive concept that takes the realization of certain objectives into view. With cognitive error the crux is one of failing to realize the truth of things, of answering our questions correctly. With practical error the issue is one of satisfying some need or desire of ours. And with judgmental error we misconstrue the worth of things. But in every case error is the same sort of thing: a matter of counterproductivity, of a shortfall or deficit in regard to success in achieving what are—or should be—our purposes.

Not only individual actions but entire processes and procedures for belief establishment can be erroneous. Just this is the case with those who are enmeshed in fallacies of reasoning of any sort. One can thus err not only in point of some specific belief, action, or evaluation but also in regard to the general way in which one proceeds in these matters. An individual who inclines to a certain generic fallacy in forming his beliefs can eventually come to see "the error of his ways." Such systemic errors are, of course, more serious because, like Shakespearean sorrows, they "come not single spies, but in battalions."

To be sure, error is not always all that serious. After all, errors are commonplace even in relation to mere games. In baseball one speaks of "hits, runs, and errors"; in tennis one speaks of "forced and unforced errors." The point is generally one of plays or moves that fail in their intended objective—generally, but not always. Suppose that whenever the light turns green you are to throw the left-hand switch, and the right-hand one whenever it turns red. But suppose further that by some quirk of fate you are enmeshed in a red-green and right-left confusion. You will thus nevertheless function perfectly since the errors you make cancel each other out so that you act with perfect success. What we have here is a "comedy of errors" of sorts, for in some circumstances error can be a pretty funny thing.

The ancient Stoics taught the strange-sounding precept that all moral errors (sins, transgressions, *peccata*, *hamartêmata*) are equal: *isa ta hamartêmata*.[1] And in a way this seems correct: once we are off the mark, we are . . . well, off the mark. Wrong is wrong, and false is false. Yet there is something odd about error egalitarianism, something reminiscent of the repugnant stance that one might be hanged for a sheep or for a lamb. The fact of error is there either way. But the *gravity* of error is something else again. For errors are not created equal. The seriousness of error is a matter of degree, of more or less. However, it is important in this context to distinguish between the *extent* of error and its *gravity*. Extent has to do with how wide off the mark a mistake happens to be. When John is in Brussels, do I put him in Paris or in Pago Pago? Gravity, by contrast, is a matter of seriousness of consequences. My failure to put John at the scene of the crime is equally serious whether I put him ten or one thousand miles off.

The magnitude of an error depends on two factors, its *extent* and its *gravity*. Extent is a matter of the range of issues involved in an error: its substantive ramifications. It stands correlative to the scale of the requisite corrections: to the volume and scope of what must be done to put matters right. Gravity is a matter of the magnitude of consequences. A cognitive error is serious to the extent that it carries further errors in its wake, be they themselves practical or merely cognitive. And practical error is serious to the extent that the actions involved result in harm or other misfortune, whence the expression "a fatal error." The gravity of error is thus a matter of its consequences: mistaken beliefs in the one case and outright harm in the other.

When people fall into it through some flaw or failing on their part, the error at issue is said to be *culpable*; otherwise it is inadvertent—as, for example, when one misreads somebody's very poor handwriting. The individual who believes or acts on patently inadequate and insufficient grounds errs culpably, unlike, say, the inadvertence of one who accepts something on the say-so of an otherwise reliable authority. An agent who is deceived by misinformation provided by another will certainly *be in error* about things, but such error is never culpable for that agent—not, at least, as long as the circumstances are not such that "he ought to know better." Again, the erroneous judgments made by someone in the wake of optical illusions will not in general be considered culpable errors as long as circumstances are not such that the deception ought to be obvious to any sensible person.

COGNITIVE ERROR

Error rears its ugly head in every department of human affairs: our choices can go wrong on every front. Cognitive errors arise in matters of knowledge, evaluative errors in matters of judgment, practical errors in matters of action. The prospect of error lurks throughout the whole landscape of human affairs.

Incorrectness of belief is a matter of outright falsity. Mere insufficiency—imprecision, inexactness, vagueness, indefiniteness, and the like—does not constitute actual error, so not every failure to be faithfully true to reality is an error. Josiah Royce maintained that "The conditions that determine the possibility of error must themselves be absolute truth."[2] Such a contention can bear a generic construal:

> The contention "Error is sometimes possible" cannot but be true.

This must be so because if, per impossibilia, the claim in question were not true, it itself would constitute an error. Alternatively, Royce's thesis also admits of a specific construal:

> If this particular contention P is to be in error, then this must be so, because certain specific conditions prevent its being true (specifically, the conditions involved in the realization of its denial not-P).

This contention must also necessarily be so, given the involvement of error in untruth. Thus with either construal, Royce's thesis of the inextricable intertwining of error with truth holds good. In acknowledging the reality of error one cannot avoid acknowledging the reality of truth as well.

To be sure, accepting p can be an error even when p is true. To say "Accepting p on his say-so was an error" will be in order when I discover him to be untrustworthy even if p is true. And someone who accepts something when all the available evidence points in the opposite direction commits a mistake even if what he believes turns out to be so. All this points to the important difference between *procedural* error and substantive error. The former consists of reaching the wrong result, the latter of going about things in an inappropriate way. The person who operates by sheer guessing, or who looks to his garage mechanic for medical advice, is entrapped in a procedural error. This is not undone as such even if the result should chance to be appropriate. While procedural error is apt to issue in substantive error as well, it is not inevitable that it should do so. The flaw of procedural error lies not in the necessarily incorrectness of its result but rather in its total unreliability. This distinction between substantive and procedural error thus functions similarly in both the cognitive realm and the practical realm.

When a correct judgment results despite the commission of a performatory error, we speak of this success as occurring "by a fluke." To say this is not, however, to say that no error has occurred, but rather to indicate that a successful result was achieved *despite* the occurrence of that (performatory) error. But would one not rather be right for the wrong reasons than err on the basis of plausible ones? That is a complex question that admits of no general answer. It all depends on the conditions and circumstances of the particular case and on the seriousness of the error at issue. Ideally, we would want to err neither in substance nor in process, and deciding on the least of the evils is always complicated.

Some theorists maintain that cognitive error is always the product of the misuse of our faculties. However, optical illusions that invite incorrect judgments regarding the size, shape, or structure of objects represents a source of error that is innocent in this regard. Again, when all the information at our disposal points in the wrong direction—has an inherent bias toward some falsehood or other—there is no cognitive impropriety in "connecting the dots" to a conclusion that happens to be incorrect. We live in a world without absolute guarantees and have no foolproof assurance that trying our best to do the right thing will lead to the right result.

Why does such a thing as cognitive error exist at all in this world of ours? Basically, because there are two fundamental failings in human cognitive capability, namely, *incapacity* in point of access to information and *incompetence* in point of information processing. Our condition in the world is such that we have to answer many questions on the basis of incomplete information, affording an opportunity for haste, carelessness, bias, and a vast array of other factors to lead our beliefs awry.

It is one thing to realize *that* a certain claim is in error and quite another to understand *how* and *why* this is so. You need not know much about the moon to recognize that the assertion that it is made of green cheese is erroneous. But to grasp the erroneousness of this error—to know *how* it goes wrong—you must know a good deal more about the matter. And, so, as R. G. Collingwood rightly stressed, refuting a false theory does not carry us back to the starting point of ignorance on the matter because we have, or should have, learned something in the process.[3] The fact of it is that knowledge can only advance across a battlefield strewn with eliminated errors. As the aficionado of detective stories well knows, at every stage of a complex inquiry there looms a host of plausible possibilities whose truth and falsity can only be distinguished with the wisdom of hindsight. There will, to be sure, be some beliefs that are exempt from error. For one thing, error cannot arise where there just is no objective fact of the matter—as is the case, for example, with the·question of just how many grains of sand it takes to make a pile.

PRACTICAL ERROR

Practical error is in general something counterproductive to an agent's *intentions* but not necessarily to that agent's *interests*. If I mistakenly turn right instead of left or say *Jane* where I meant *John*, it is perfectly possible that this slip-up averted disaster and engendered splendid consequences. This advantageous result, however, does not preclude the fact that I acted in error. When an error produces a positive result, this does not alter its status as such.

Is it an error to use a device that malfunctions? In general no. But only when the malfunction occurs in circumstances when it could or should have been foreseen—or where the stake is so great that its mere probability should not have been risked—can one speak of error in real cases. Obviously, the effect can be exactly the same irrespective of whether a human error (not filling the tank) or a mechanical malfunction (the tank's springing a leak) causes a certain unfortunate result (running out of fuel). The crucial difference lies only in the sort of preventative steps that need to be taken (instruction in the case of humans, inspection in that of machines).

The relation to objectives is accordingly crucial for error, both those objectives we *do* have and those we *should* have, such as physical or psychological well-being. The former sort of error relates to *optional* ends; the latter to *mandatory* ends that people in general ought to have, even though many (perverts and psychopaths included) do not actually have. Some ends and aims are not optional but inherent in the human situation as such. Food, shelter, clothing, safeguarding when young, companionship and mutual aid—these are only a few examples of our needs, that is, objectives that are mandated for us by our mode of emplacement within the world's scheme of things. Other prime examples of these mandatory ends relate to issues of ethics and morality. And here errors stretch across a wide spectrum, from minor transgressions to outright sins.

Are there such things as *unavoidable* errors? Certainly not in cognitive matters, seeing that in this sphere error can always be avoided by simply suspending judgment: in accepting nothing we accept nothing wrong. But in matters of practice things stand differently. For here you can become trapped in a dilemma where you are damned if you do and damned if you don't. But the larger lesson here is that this sort of thing can only occur as the consequence of past error. Thus someone who has undertaken incompatible commitments may find himself in a position where he must either break a promise made to X or break one made to Y. But this dilemma is the consequence of a past error—namely, making those potentially incompatible promises: having already made a promise to X, it was clearly an error—a moral error—to make a potentially incompatible promise to Y.

EVALUATIVE ERROR

Homo sapiens is also *Homo valuens*: humans are evaluative animals. We have a natural tendency to take an evaluative stance of pro or con toward virtually everything. Most of the things we see we view in a positive or negative light. When reading a newspaper, every development reported upon strikes us as either good or bad: if we marked those we view positively in green and those we view negatively in red, few items would remain in colorless neutrality (perhaps the table of tides and the shipping news, unless we happen to be sea people ourselves). Our minds tend to spread the coloration of approval-or-disapproval across pretty well everything that they touch.

To be sure, some evaluative questions relate to what is entirely a matter of taste, of sheer subjective preference rather than inherently objective preferability. And here, too, there is no prospect of error. (That *X finds* parts of *Don Quixote* boring is a flat-out fact; but that parts of *Don Quixote are* boring—so that sensible people *ought* to find them so—does not seem to constitute a clear-cut fact one way or the other.) However, with many evaluative matters error is indeed possible, though here we tend to talk of *errors of judgment* rather than errors, flat out.

COMMISSION VERSUS OMISSION

Evaluative errors excepted, errors come in two basic forms: those of omission and those of commission. Errors of omission are failures to accept true facts in the cognitive case and failures to do what is circumstantially required in the practical. Errors of commission lie in accepting falsehoods in the cognitive case, performing counterproductive actions in the practical. Errors of omission are often called errors of the first kind (type I errors), while errors of commission are referred to as errors of the second kind (type II errors). In cognitive contexts, errors of omission consist in giving partial and incomplete answers to the questions at issue. Most serious here are *misleading* answers, which, while in themselves correct, nevertheless embody suggestions and implications that point in an entirely wrong direction and could or would be corrected if only the omitted information were also supplied.

In practical goal-directed contexts, errors of omission consist in failing, for whatever reason, to do those things required to facilitate realization of the goal at issue. This is, of course, most serious in the case of mandatory goals, be they prudential or moral. It is, or should be, clear that errors (and sins) of omission can be every bit as serious as those of commission.

The well-known controversy between William James and William Kingdon Clifford yields an instructive lesson for epistemology through leading us to recognize that as regards the theory of knowledge (as in other ways) we live in an imperfect world. The ultimate ideal of absolute perfection is outside our grasp: the prospect of proceeding in ways wholly free from the risk of error is not attainable in this epistemic dispensation where there is an inherent trade-off between errors of commission and omission. They stand in inseparable coordination: any realistically workable mechanism of cognition can only avoid errors of the first kind (excluding truths) at the expense of incurring errors of the second kind (including untruths). The situation is as portrayed in figure 1.1. As the situation of point (1) indicates, if we insist upon adopting an epistemic policy that allows no type II errors and admits no untruths at all, then we are constrained to all-out scepticism: we can accept nothing and are thereby involved in a total exclusion from the whole realm of truths. The situation of point (3), on the other hand, indicates that, as we insist with increasing stridency upon reducing the exclusion of truths so as to curtail

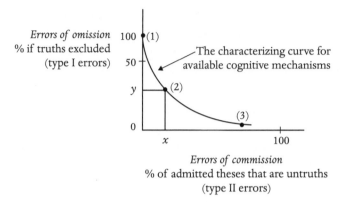

Figure 1.1. The trade-off between the two kinds of error

type I errors, we are compelled to an increasingly gullible policy that allows the goats to wander through the gate alongside the sheep. It is the happy medium of point (2) that we must strive to realize.

What we confront here is clearly a calculus-like minimax problem where we strive for the optimal balance of truths attained relative to errors excluded. However, the idealized schematic of achieving the whole truth (no errors of omission) and nothing but the truth (no errors of commission) is simply not part of the achievable realities of the human situation. As we become more enterprising and reduce our involvement in errors of omission, we are unavoidably bound to become involved in more errors of commission. In the conduct of our cognitive affairs, as in other departments of life, we must do the best we can in the circumstances: what one might abstractly think of as the absolute ideal is simply not attainable in this mundane dispensation.

There is an extensive and diversified terminology of cognitive error. There are misjudgments and misunderstandings, over- and underestimates, misestimates, and so on. A comparable situation prevails on the performatory side, where we find mispronunciation in speaking, misspelling in writing, mis-hits in tennis, and mis-throws in baseball. Many errors of this general sort acquire special nomenclature—"double faults" in tennis, over- or undercooking in cuisine, Freudian-slips in communication, and the like. Benjamin Franklin the printer looked on the mistakes of his life as so many errata and wished he could add corrigenda to his life history.

MORE ON COGNITIVE ERROR

Cognitive error becomes common because truth is comparatively rare. After all, every true belief stands coordinate with not only its unique false contradictory but also a myriad of equally false contraries. When was Napoleon born? Why did he leave Elba? With such questions there is but one correct answer with a profusion of incorrect alternatives. And this means that the opportunity for error is limitless.

The quest for information exempt from the possibility of error—for absolutely certain knowledge—has been on the agenda of philosophy at least since Plato's day. The following are prime candidates for error-proof belief:

> *Elemental logical facts,* such as "If *p*-and-*q* obtains, then *p* does."

> *Elementary mathematical facts,* such as "2 + 2 = 4" or "A sphere has no corners."

> *Definitional facts* that either form parts of definitions or are obvious consequences of them.

> *Elementary observable facts,* such as "Orange resembles red more than it does blue."

> *Reports of personal experience and subjective impression:* "That leaf looks green to me," or "I am under the impression that that is a cat over there." (Note that all such

statements are subjectively about oneself rather than
objectively about how the world is constituted.)

The drawback of all such error-proof facts is that none of them is able
to provide substantial information about how things stand in the
world. Such error-proof facts are also often characterized as being
"foolproof" subject to the idea that the facts at issue are sufficiently
simple to be at the disposal of the simple considered as being "things
that any fool knows." They pay the price for their error-resistant certainty in terms of a sacrifice of substantial informativeness.

Knowledge is inherently coordinated with truth claims. It makes
no sense to say "*p* is true, but I don't know it to be so" with any specific
proposition *p* in view. Nor, again, to say "I know that *p*, but it may possibly not be true." Note, however, that this differs from "I know that *p*
is true, but it *could* possibly not be so (if the world were different)." To
claim knowledge is to maintain truth. All the same, with regard to
our knowledge claims, as with pretty much everything else, we may
well be mistaken. We do, and must, recognize all too clearly that
much of what we claim as knowledge is merely *putative* knowledge,
and that much of our putative knowledge is in fact error.

In speaking of a cognitive error one must be very specific about
just what the issue at hand is. Take the case of an optical illusion,
such as the straight stick that looks bent when held under the water
at an angle. While it is certainly an error to say that it *is* bent, to say
that it *looks* bent is not. The issue of being versus appearing is thus
crucial for the correctness of the issue of straight versus bent.

Some systemic failings are linked specifically to cognitive errors:
a tendency to jump to conclusions, for example, or gullibility. Others
will operate adversely across the whole range of error, cognitive and
practical alike: carelessness, heedlessness, or forgetfulness. Persons
who exhibit such failings to a more than ordinary extent are said to
be error prone.

Can one regard one's own beliefs as being in error? Certainly not in specific cases. If I regarded p's acceptance as an error, then I ipso facto would not—and coherently could not—also include it among my beliefs. All the same, at the level of generality we realize full well that we are not perfect in cognitive matters. We have no choice but to acknowledge our fallibility. One cannot coherently say or think "I believe p to be the case but am mistaken about it." Categorizing what one accepts here and now as erroneous is infeasible in view of the fact that "acceptance" here means acceptance *as true*. The retrospectivity of a wisdom of hindsight is, of course, something else again. There is no problem with "I believed p to be the case but was mistaken about it." This sort of thing is all too common. We realize *that* we succumb to error despite the inability to pinpoint *where* we do so.

Thus it is nowise absurd or incoherent but the very reverse to think that *some* of one's beliefs could turn out to be mistaken. It is in fact impossible that I should be mistaken about this. For if (per impossible) I were mistaken here, then this very fact would establish the correctness of my belief. Someone who deems herself fallible in that some of her beliefs might be wrong cannot possibly err in all of those beliefs. (By contrast, as long as one acts at all, it becomes possible that all of one's actions could be practical error in that *everything* one does will be counterproductive vis-à-vis one's perfectly appropriate ends and objectives.)

That an error has been made is something that often only comes to light with the wisdom of hindsight, since what was done "seemed like a good idea at the time." (A classic instance of this was turning the Titanic to miss that iceberg: hitting it head-on would only have caused a large dent in its prow, whereas sideswiping it created a long underwater gash across several watertight compartments. But who could have known?)

The most extensive and longstanding discussion of error in philosophy has revolved around fallacies, a discussion that has flourished since the days of Aristotle's *Sophistical Refutations*.[4] Most of this material falls into the realm of epistemology, because what is involved pivots on misreasonings that extract *unwarranted* conclusions from actually or assumptively available information. Fallacies are generic processes of reasoning that are liable to lead to erroneous results (even if not inevitably bound to do so).[5] A paradigm instance of a formal fallacy is the fallacy of affirming the consequent—a course of reasoning whose format stands as follows:

$$p \rightarrow q$$
$$q$$
$$\overline{\therefore p}$$

Such reasoning is clearly fallacious, seeing that it uses such obviously unacceptable arguments as the following:

If you are in New York, you are in America
You are in America.

Therefore: You are in New York

Fallacious reasoning is not, of course, the only avenue to epistemic error: sheer conclusiveness, reckless conclusion-leaping, and foolish credulity are other prime prospects. But the prominent role of logic in philosophy has brought fallacy into the forefront here. In actual practice formal fallacies are often enthymemes that tacitly assume certain plausible-seeming but possibly false substantive presuppositions. For example, in the preceding case one may be tempted to see that indication as holding in reverse as well. And should this prove to be so, that argument would be salvageable. Formal fallacies illustrate the point that error avoidance can be inadvertent. Thus if you reject p but accept q and thereby also accept $p \lor q$, while q is in fact false but p true, then you manage to avoid being mistaken in regard to $p \lor q$.

But this is entirely accidental, being the result of two now mutually canceling errors.

Is error always corrigible? Certainly so in the case of substantive cognitive error where the issue is simply one of information mismanagement. For here there is, by hypothesis, a fact of the matter, and the error at issue can be corrected by indicating this fact. However, practical error is something else again. For it relates to counterproductive actions occurring on the world's stage. And such occurrences can be overtaken by the course of events so that the counterproductivity involved can no longer be corrected because a point of no return has been reached. For example, although sins can be regretted and atoned for with contrition, they generally cannot be erased nor undone.

FURTHER ASPECTS OF ERROR

Can we frail mortals ever be exempt from error? Can we become literally infallible? Here, again, distinctions need to be made. The ancient Greeks differentiated between that which is so by nature *(phusis)* and that which is so by human convention *(nomos)*. Now, by convention we can certainly become infallible—as with any court of final appeal in matters of law. But authentic and natural infallibility is not for us; at this level infallibility is the exclusive preserve of an omniscient God. Making mistakes is certainly something people rarely intend to do. But all the same, as long as there is such a thing as self-deception, it will not be entirely inappropriate to say that people can err deliberately in certain sorts of circumstances—in particular, those in which being in the right would simply be too painful.

Can someone err deliberately? Can a person knowingly and deliberately believe and endorse something that he deems to be false? After all, if by "believe" one means believe *to be true* and by endorse we mean "endorse as being true" (and it is surely this that is at issue here), then deliberate error becomes something altogether problematic. And this is so not so much because we deem people to be rational but rather because we ourselves propose to behave rationally. It is this rationality *on our own part* that precludes our maintaining, on the one hand, that

> X believes p to be true (or X accepts p as a truth),

and, on the other hand,

> X deems p to be false (or X regards p as a falsehood).

For were we to say this, it would transpire that there is nonconsistency all right—but on *our* part, not on *X*'s.

ERROR AND THE PURSUIT OF KNOWLEDGE

The risk of error is unavoidable throughout the cognitive enterprise, and the control of error is a key aspect of rational inquiry. Since error cannot be eliminated from human affairs, we have little choice but to make the most of it. Our only route to cognitive progress proceeds along a pathway paved with error—we are creatures to whom truth becomes available only by risking error.[6] Our knowledge grows only by eliminating error. Nevertheless, the elimination of error need not do much in and of itself to grease the wheels of knowledge. "What did you think about while you were waiting for her?" "Well—not George Washington; not the Treaty of Versailles; not the square root of two." All this is true enough, and each item eliminates a possible mistake. But none of it brings us any closer to obtaining the real answer.

The role of error-correction in the theory of scientific method was initially explored by Charles Sanders Peirce.[7] It is stressed throughout the work of Karl R. Popper and it has more recently been instructively developed and amplified by Deborah Mayo,[8] whose work elucidates the fruitful and substantive linkage between traditional philosophical approaches and the error-geared reasoning of contemporary statistical theory. Clearly, the *via negativa* of error elimination is not the most promising way to knowledge acquisition. But, nevertheless, one of the best and most effective standards by which to test any proposed method or process of knowledge production lies in its capacity to minimize the chances of error.

ERROR AND CREATIVE THINKING

Correct thinking characterizes what is the case; error misrepresents this by affirming what is not. But does not error thereby engender something new and different, over and above what really is? Is error not in a way creative? This question is part of a broader issue. Can thought—veridical or not—create objects? Is there anything deserving of the name *thing* or *object* that can be created by thought? The plausible candidates here are listed in table 1.1.[9]

In scrutinizing table 1.1, a significant omission comes to view. For the idea emerges that *thought creates no authentic, identifiable, concrete*

Table 1.1. Objects created by thought

Concrete items (located in space time)

    The specific episodes of thinking by particular individuals.

    The general collectivity of thinking by members of a group (a society or culture, etc.).

Abstract items

    The thought-items (theses, propositions, theories, hypotheses, ideas, plans, plots, etc.) that figure in the aforementioned concrete acts of thinking.

    The thought-artifacts (languages, words, alphabets, norms) that constitute the machinery that figures in the aforementioned acts of thinking.

---

objects apart from those episodic events of thinking themselves and their concatenations. But what then of the objects that figure in hypothesis, dreams, and delusions: the Easter Bunny and present king of France? Are these not creatures of thought? In fact they are not. For what thought creates in not such objects but merely the *ideas* of such objects. The putative objects at issue do not exist in themselves. Of course those ideas exist, but they are something abstract. The objects themselves are among the missing. After all, putative concreteness is not the real thing. The tabulation accordingly reflects what is an appropriate conclusion: Acts of thinking themselves apart, thought creates no concreta, only abstracta.

I tell my class, "Imagine a fat man in that doorway." The students obey my instruction—all proceed to think as it demands. But now how many imaginary men are there in the doorway? Thirty of them—one for each imagining student? Or just one of them, each imagining the same fat man? What if they are imagined differently— sometimes with a shirt and tie, sometimes with just a turtleneck? Does being imagined differently make them different? Does being imagined alike make them one and the same? All these questions are nonsense. You cannot count imaginary men because they lack individualized identity. The imagining of a man does not yield a definite item—an imaginary man. Unlike any actual man whatsoever, that "imaginary man" does not answer to a completely detailed description: what is at issue is schematic and is no particular individual with a definite identity of its own.

Consider the contrast between something real and something merely putative—say, between Napoleon *(N)* and Napoleon-as-*X*-thinks-him-to-be *(N/X),* that is, Napoleon as he was and *X*'s conception of him. Obviously, the things that are true of the *real* object (Napoleon) need not be true of the *putative* object (Napoleon-as-*X*-thinks-him-to-be). A discrepancy will occur whenever *X* is in error (be it in omission or commission). We cannot equate the two: they have different properties. The actual N just may not answer to X's conception of him. And yet the individuals at issue are identical— were they not, there would be no error. So complications arise here.

Worse yet, what if what is at issue is not a "mere misconception" but actually a case of mistaken identity? In particular, what if N/X is some nonexistent M and thus something altogether different from N—say, "the Man in the Iron Mask"? Clearly, N/X may not be identical with N at all. We would be well advised here to speak not of "X's conception of N," but of "X's altogether mistaken impression that N is the Man in the Iron Mask." In the end, X's conception of Napoleon is a creature of X's. Were there no thinkers, the world's reals would still exist; but misconceptions about them would not.

Yet while thinking—however deluded—is undeniably a part of reality, nevertheless, what is at issue will often as not be more products of thought's own activities and thus not real things as such but at most and best only ideas of things. And these ideas will always have an element of schematic abstraction about them and fail to be concretely identified items! Its own proceedings apart, thought is inert with respect to substantive reality. In and of itself it does not produce definite objects—or at least not objects different from those thoughts themselves. And since the thematic content of our thinking remains schematic, it does not, cannot, create a definite object. Authentic objects are by nature individuals. Those putatively thought-created so-called objects are no more than mere ideas of objects that, as such, are mere abstractions rather than substantial objects. Yet even here error can make inroads, since even thought-objects such as Alexius Meinong's round square can be enmeshed in inherent mistakes.

✕ 2 ✕

The Dialectic of Ignorance and Error

THE CORRIGIBILITY OF CONCEPTIONS

One can err only where one has prior knowledge, maintains one recent author.[1] But this is very questionable. If the idea never even occurs to me that the paragraph I am reading contains a coded message, then I am in error in blithely seeing it as a normal text. But one would hardly say that I am committing an error by doing so. Errors of omission simply occur rather than get committed. We can certainly *commit* errors, but erroneous impressions and inclinations can also take us unawares, as errors of omission are apt to do.

In deliberating about error it is necessary to distinguish between the correctness of our particular *claims* about things and our very *ideas* of them—between a true or correct *contention,* on the one hand, and a true *conception,* on the other. To make a true contention about a thing, we need merely get *some one particular fact* about it right. But to have a true conception of the thing, we must get *all of the important facts* about it right.[2] With a correct contention (statement) about a thing, all is well if we get the single relevant aspect of it right, but with a correct conception of it *we must get the essentials right—we must have the correct overall picture.* This duality of error as between false belief and erroneous conception ("applying to one thing the definition proper to another") goes back at least to St. Thomas Aquinas.[3]

To ensure the correctness of our conception of a thing we would have to be sure—as we very seldom are—that nothing further can possibly come along to upset our view of just what its important features are and just what their character is. The qualifying conditions for true conceptions are thus far more demanding than those for true claims. No doubt, in the fifth century BCE Anaximander of Miletus may have made many correct contentions about the sun—for example, that it is not a mass of burning stuff pulled about on its circuit by a deity with a chariot drawn by a winged horse. But Anaximander's *conception* of the sun (as the flaming spoke of a great wheel of fire encircling the earth) was seriously wrong.

With conceptions—unlike propositions or contentions—incompleteness means incorrectness, or at any rate *presumptive* incorrectness. A conception that is based on substantially incomplete data must be assumed to be at least partially incorrect. If we can decipher only half the inscription, our conception of its over-all content must be largely conjectural—and thus must be presumed to contain an admixture of error. When our information about something is incomplete, obtaining an overall picture of the thing at issue becomes a matter of theorizing, or guesswork, however sophisticatedly executed. And then we have little alternative but to suppose that this over-all picture falls short of being wholly correct in various (unspecifiable) ways. With conceptions, falsity can thus emerge from errors of omission as well of commission that result from the circumstance that the information at our disposal is merely incomplete rather than actually erroneous (as will have to be the case with false contentions).

The incompleteness of our knowledge does not, of course, *ensure* its incorrectness—after all, even a single isolated belief can represent a truth. But it does strongly *invite* it. For if our information about some object is incomplete, then it is bound to be unrepresentative of the objective makeup-as-a-whole so that a judgment regarding that object is liable to be false. The situation is akin to that depicted in John Godfrey Saxe's splendid poem "The Blind Men and the Elephant," which tells the story of certain blind sages, those

> Six men of Indostan,
> To learning much inclined,
> Who went to see the elephant,
> (Though all of them were blind).

One sage touched the elephant's "broad and sturdy side" and declared the beast to be "very like a wall." The second, who had felt its tusk, announced the elephant to resemble a spear. The third, who took the elephant's squirming trunk in his hands, compared it to a snake; while the fourth, who put his arm around the elephant's knee, was sure that the animal resembled a tree. A flapping ear convinced another that the elephant had the form of a fan; while the sixth blind man, having taken hold of the tail, thought that it had the form of a rope.

> And so these men of Indostan,
> Disputed loud and long;
> Each in his own opinion
> Exceeding stiff and strong:
> Though each was partly in the right,
> And all were in the wrong.

The lesson is clear. The incompleteness of object-descriptive statements certainly does not entail their incorrectness: incomplete information does not ensure false belief. But it does ensure inadequate understanding, since at the level of generality there will be too many gaps that need filling in. An inadequate or incomplete description of something is not thereby false; the statements we make about it may be perfectly true as far as they go. But an inadequate or incomplete conception of a thing is *eo ipso* one that we have no choice but to presume to be incorrect as well,[4] because we cannot justifiably take the stance that this incompleteness relates only to inconsequentiate matters and touches nothing important, thereby distorting our conception of things so that errors of commission result. There are just too many alternative ways in which reality can round out an incomplete account to warrant confidence in the exclusion of error. Accordingly, our conceptions of particular things should be viewed not just as cognitively *open-ended,* but as *corrigible* as well.

It is important to be clear about just what point is at issue here. It is certainly not being denied that people do indeed know many truths about things—for example, that Caesar did correctly know many things about his sword. Rather, what is being maintained is not only that there were many things he did not know about it (such as that it contained tungsten) but also that his over-all conception of it was in many ways inadequate and in some ways incorrect.

This vulnerability of our putative knowledge of the world in the face of potential error is exhibited rather than *refuted* by a consideration of scientific knowledge. For this knowledge is by no means as secure and absolute as we like to think. The history of science is the history of changes of mind about the truth of things. The science of the present is an agglomeration of corrections of the science of the past. Throughout the cognitive enterprise—and, above all, throughout the sciences—much of what we vaunt as "our knowledge" is no more than our *best estimate* of the truth of things. And we recognize in our heart of hearts that this putative truth in fact incorporates a great deal of error. There is every reason to believe that where scientific knowledge is concerned further knowledge does not just supplement but generally corrects our knowledge-in-hand, so that the incompleteness of our information implies its presumptive incorrectness as well. We must come to terms with the fact that, at any rate, at the scientific level of generality and precision, *each* of our accepted beliefs *may* eventuate as false and *many* of our accepted beliefs *will* eventuate as false. The road to scientific progress is paved with acknowledged error.

But if we acknowledge the presence of error within the body of our putative knowledge, then why not simply correct it? The salient lesson here is conveyed by what has become known under the rubric of *the preface paradox,* whose jest is as follows: An author's preface reads, "I realize that, because of the complex nature of the issues involved, the text of the book is bound to contain some errors. For these I now apologize in advance." There is clearly something paradoxical going on with this otherwise far-from-outlandish disclaimer because the statements of the main text are flatly asserted and thereby claimed as truths yet the preface statement affirms that some of them are false. Despite an acknowledgment of a collective error, there is a claim to distributive correctness. Our author obviously cannot have it both ways.[5] In reading the preface, the impatient reader may want to exclaim, "You silly author—if there are errors, then why not just correct them?" But here's the rub: The author would correct these errors if only he could tell where and what they were. But this is exactly what he does not know. They may be in full view, but they are not identifiable as such. As *error,* they are totally invisible. And exactly this situation of the preface paradox is paradigmatic for the situation of science as regards its errors.

The very concept of a *thing* that underlies our discourse about this world's realities is thus based on a certain sort of tentativity and fallibilism—the implicit recognition that our own personal or even communal conception of things may well be wrong and is, in any case, inadequate. At the bottom of our belief about things at the level of generality and precision at issue in science there always is—or should be—a certain wariness that recognizes the possibility of error. But, of course, none of this unravels its legitimacy and utility.

COMMUNICATIVE PARALLAX

The fact that real things have hidden depths, that they are cognitively opaque, has important ramifications that reach to the very heart of the theory of communication. Any particular thing—the moon, for example—is such that two related but critically different versions of it can be contemplated: the moon, the actual moon as it "really" is, and the moon as somebody (you or I or the Babylonians) conceives of it.

The crucial fact to note in this connection is that it is virtually always the thing itself that we *intend* to communicate or think (that is, self-communicate) about, the thing *as it is,* and not the thing *as somebody conceives of it.* Yet we cannot but recognize the justice of Kant's teaching that the "I think" (I maintain, assert) is an ever-present implicit accompaniment of every claim or contention that we make. This factor of attributability dogs our every assertion and opens up the unavoidable prospect of "getting it wrong"—and not right about the wrong moon but wrong about the one and only moon.

Ambitious intentions or pretensions to the contrary notwithstanding, all that one can ever actually manage to bring off in one's purportedly fact-assertive discourse is to convey what one thinks or conceives to be so. I can readily distinguish the features of (what I take to be) "the real moon" from those of "the moon as *you* conceive of it," but I cannot distinguish them from those of "the moon as *I* conceive of it." And when *I* maintain, "The moon is roughly spherical," all that I have successfully managed to deliver to you in terms of actual information is, "Rescher maintains that the moon is roughly spherical." To get from this to the moon itself you need to endorse a contention that is squarely about me—that is to say, that I am a suitable source of information where the moon is concerned. And there is nothing that can be done to alter this circumstance. My claims do no more than convey what I think to be so, no matter how loudly I bang on the table.[6] If you bind me by the injunction, "Tell me something about the Eiffel Tower, but please do not put before me your beliefs or convictions regarding it; just give me facts about the thing itself rather than presenting any parts of your conception of it," you condemn me to the silence of the Lockean *je ne sais quoi*.

THE COMMUNICATIVE IRRELEVANCE OF INADEQUATE CONCEPTIONS

The acknowledgment of potential error is communicatively irrelevant. Our fundamental intention is to take real objects to be at issue, objects as they are in themselves, our potentially idiosyncratic and erroneous conceptions of them quite aside; it is fundamental because it overrides all of our other intentions when we enter upon the communicative venture. Without this conventionalized intention, we would not be able to convey information—or misinformation—to one another about a shared "objective" world. We could never establish communicative contact about a common objective item of discussion if our discourse were geared not to the things themselves but to the things as conceived of in terms of our own specific information about them.

Any pretensions to the predominance, let alone the correctness, of our own conceptions regarding the furniture of this realm must be put aside in the context of communication. The fundamental intention to deal with the objective order of this "real world" is crucial. If our assertoric commitments did not transcend the information we ourselves have on hand, we would never be able to "get in touch" with others about a shared objective world. No claim is made for the *primacy* of our conceptions, or for the *correctness* of our conceptions, or even for the mere *agreement* of our conceptions with those of others. The fundamental intention to discuss "the thing itself" predominates and overrides any mere dealing with the thing as we ourselves conceive of it.

This ever-operative contrast between "the thing itself" and "the thing as we ourselves take it to be" means that we are never in a position to claim definitive finality for our conception of a thing. We are never entitled to claim to have exhausted it *au fond* in cognitive regards—that we have managed to bring it wholly within our epistemic grasp. For to make this claim would, in effect, be to *identify* "the thing itself" in terms of "our own conception of it," an identification that would effectively remove the former item (the thing itself) from the stage of consideration as an independent entity in its own right by endowing our conception with decisively determinative force. And this would lead straightaway to the unpleasant result of a cognitive solipsism that would preclude reference to intersubjectively identifiable particulars, and would thus block the possibility of interpersonal communication. It is a fundamental presupposition of communicative discourse that we are engaged in stating what we think to be true about the objects we take to be at issue—that we endeavor to characterize them as they are and not merely as we think them to be.

Seen in *this* light, the key point may be put as follows: It is indeed a presupposition of effective communicative discourse about a thing that we purport (claim and intend) to make objectively true statements about it. But it is *not* required for such discourse that we purport to have a true or even adequate conception of the thing at issue. On the contrary, we must deliberately abstain from any claim that our own conception is definitive if we are to engage successfully in discourse. We deliberately put the whole matter of conception aside—abstracting from the question of the agreement of my conception with yours, and all the more from the issue of which of us has the right conception.[7]

If we were to set up our own conception as somehow definitive and decisive, we would at once erect a grave impediment to the prospect of successful communication with one another. Communication could then only proceed retrospectively with the wisdom of hindsight. It would be realized only in the implausible case that extensive exchange indicates that there has been an *identity* of conceptions all along. We would then learn only by experience—at the end of a long process of wholly tentative and provisional exchange. And we would always stand on very shaky ground. For no matter how far we push our inquiry into the issue of an identity of conceptions, the prospect of a divergence lying just around the corner—waiting to be discovered if only we pursued the matter just a bit further—can never be precluded. One could never advance the issue of the identity of focus past the status of a more or less well-grounded *assumption.* And then any so-called communication is no longer an exchange of information but a tissue of frail conjectures. The communicative enterprise would become a vast inductive project, a complex exercise in theory-building leading tentatively and provisionally toward something that, in fact, the imputational groundwork of our language enables us to presuppose from the very outset.[8]

The fact that we need not agree on our conceptions of things means, *a fortiori,* that we need not be correct in our conceptions of things to communicate successfully about them. This points, in part, to the trivial fact that I need not agree with what you are saying to understand you. But it points also, more importantly, to the consideration that my having a conception of a thing massively different from yours will not prevent me from taking you to be talking about the same thing that I have in mind. Objectivity and referential commonality of focus are matters of initial presumption or presupposition. The issue here is not with what is understood but with what is *to be* understood (by anybody) in terms of certain generalized and communicative intentions. (The issue here is not one of *meaning* but only of *meaningfulness*.)

Our concept of a *real thing* accordingly affords a fixed point, a stable center around which communication revolves, the invariant focus of potentially diverse conceptions. What is to be determinative, decisive, definitive of the things at issue in my discourse is not my conception, or yours, or indeed anyone's conception at all. The conventionalized intention discussed above means that a coordination of conceptions is not decisive for the possibility of communication. Your statements about a thing will convey something to me even if my conception of it is altogether different from yours. To communicate we need not take ourselves to share views of the word, but only to take the stance that we share the world being discussed.

In communication regarding things we must be able to exchange information about them with our contemporaries and to transmit information about them to our successors. And we must be in a position to do this in the face of the presumption that *their* conceptions of things are not only radically different from *ours* but conceivably also rightly different. What is at issue here is not the commonplace that we do not know *everything* about anything. Rather, the key consideration is the more interesting thesis that it is a crucial precondition of the possibility of successful communication about things that we must avoid laying any claim either to the completeness or even to the ultimate correctness of our own conceptions of any of the things at issue.

It is crucial that the mechanisms of human communication should lie within the domain of human power. Now, with respect to the *meanings of words* this condition is satisfied, because this is something that we ourselves fix by custom or by fiat. But *the correctness of conceptions* is not simply a matter of human discretion; it is something that lies outside the sphere of our effective control. For a "correct conception" is akin to Spinoza's *true idea* of which he stipulates that it must "agree with its object" in circumstances where this issue of agreement may well elude us.[9] (Man proposes but does not dispose with respect to this matter of idea/actuality coordination.) We do, no doubt, *purport* our conceptions to be correct, but whether this is indeed so is something we cannot tell with assurance until "all the returns are in"—that is, never. This fact renders it critically important *that* (and understandable *why*) conceptions are communicatively irrelevant. Our discourse *reflects* our conceptions and perhaps *conveys* them, but it is not substantive *about* them. And it is this downing to realism that also opens a route to error.

Our subjective conception of things may be the vehicle of thought, but it is never the determinant of reference. *By* their very nature, conceptions are too personal—and thus potentially too idiosyncratic—for our communicative needs. For communication, interpersonal and public instrumentalities are indispensably requisite. And language affords this desideratum. It provides the apparatus by which the *identity* of the referents of our discourse becomes fixed, however imperfectly we ourselves perceive their nature. (The specifications of things as enshrined in language are Kripkean "rigid designators" in an *epistemic* manner: our indicators for real-things-in-the-world are *designed* in both senses, constructed and intended to perform—insofar as possible—an invariant identificatory job across the diversified spectrum of epistemic worlds.)

How do we really know that Anaximander was talking about *our* sun? He is not here to tell us. He did not leave an elaborate discussion about his aims and purposes. How can we be so confident of what he meant to talk about? The answer is straightforward. That he is *to be taken* to be talking about *our* sun is, in the final analysis, something that turns on two very general issues in which Anaximander himself plays little if any role at all: (1) our subscription to certain generalized principles of interpretation with respect to the Greek language, and (2) the conventionalized subscription by us and ascription to other language users in general of certain fundamental communicative policies and intentions. In the face of appropriate functional equivalences we allow neither a difference in language nor a difference of "thought-worlds" to block an identity of reference.

The overarching *intention* to communicate about a common object—abandoning any and all claims to regard our own conceptions of it as definitive (decisive)—is the indispensable foundation of all communication. And this intention is not something personal and idiosyncratic—a biographical aspect of certain particular minds; it is a shared feature of "social mind," built into the use of language as a publicly available communicative resource. The wider social perspective is crucial. In subscribing to the conventionalized intention at issue, we sink "our own point of view" in the interests of entering into the wider community of fellow communicators. Only by admitting the potential distortion of one's own conceptions of things through "communicative parallax" can one manage to reach across the gulf of divergent conceptions so as to get into communicative touch with one another. In this context, the pretension-humbling stance of a cognitive Copernicanism is not only a matter of virtue but one of necessity as well. It is the price we pay for keeping the channels of communication open.

The commitment to *objectivity* is basic to our discourse with one regarding about a shared world of "real things" to which none of us has privileged access. This commitment establishes a need to "distance" ourselves from things—that is, to recognize the prospect of a discrepancy between our (potentially idiosyncratic) conceptions about them and the true character of these things as they exist objectively in "the real world." The ever-present contrast between "the thing as we view it" and "the thing as it is" is the mechanism by which this crucially important distancing is accomplished.

The information that we may have about a thing—be it real or presumptive information—is always just that: information that *we* lay claim to. We cannot but recognize that it is person-relative and, in general, person-differentiated. However, our attempts at communication and inquiry are thus undergirded by an information-transcending stance, the stance that we communally inhabit a shared world of objectively existing things, a world of "real things" amongst which we live and into which we inquire but about which we do and must presume ourselves to have only imperfect information at any and every particular stage of the cognitive venture. This is not something we learn. The "facts of experience" can never reveal it to us, and indeed would not themselves be available without it. It is something we presume or presuppose from the very outset. Its epistemic status is not that of an empirical discovery but of a presupposition whose ultimate rationale is a transcendental argument for the very possibility of communication or inquiry as we standardly conceive of them.

True enough, cognitive change carries conceptual change in its wake. But nevertheless—and this point is crucial—we have an ongoing commitment to a manifold of objective *things* that are themselves impervious to merely conceptual and cognitive change. This commitment is built into the very ground rules that govern our use of language and embody our determination to maintain the picture of a relatively stable world amidst the ever-changing panorama of people's cognitive world pictures. The continuing succession of the different states of science are all linked to a pre- or sub-scientific view of an ongoing "real world" in which we live and labor, a world portrayed rather more stably in the *lingua franca* of everyday life communication and populated by shared things whose stability amidst cognitive change is something rather *postulated* than learned. This postulation reflects the realistic stance that the things we encounter in experience are the *subject* and not the *product* of our inquiries. And it serves a supremely important function in limiting the impact of error on the practicability of interpersonal communication.[10]

$\times$ 3 $\times$

Scepticism and the Risk of Error

SCEPTICISM

How pervasive can error be? This question sends us on a visit to the all-powerful deceiver of Descartes and the Martian mind-controllers of science fiction. And so the sceptic presses the question: "How do you (ever) know that you are not in error now?" The answer is, "It all depends!" It will depend on what is at issue in that supposedly error-prone belief of mine. If it happens to be, "People sometimes err," then it just cannot possibly be in error. If it is the Cartesian, "I think; I exist," its being in error is unthinkable. If it is, "There are rocks in the world," the prospect of error is so remote that anyone who took it seriously might as well wear a label that says, "I am crazy." The prospect and likelihood of error is clearly something that is subject-matter dependent. Here, as elsewhere, reflection and experience will have to be our teachers, and we have little choice but to look to them for instruction in the topic. There will be some people who err most of the time, and doubtless all people will err some of the time. But the prospect that all people err all of the time can be dismissed out of hand.

Clearly, the ideal sort of inquiry process is one that efficiently provides certifiably correct answers to our questions so that the issue of error is effectively expelled from the scene. However, since we do not live in an ideal world, we must come to terms with the prospect of error. Therefore, it becomes desirable to seek an inquiry procedure that provides for error detection, so that even where it cannot certify truth it at least affords a means for detecting erroneous answers. Indeed, in the special case of a finite and determinate range of possibilities (where we have what might be characterized as the Agatha Christie situation, a state of affairs also envisioned in Francis Bacon's idea of eliminative induction), such a procedure meets the conditions characterized above as ideal. For in these circumstances there will come into operation what might be characterized as the Sherlock Holmes principle: "When you have eliminated the impossible, whatever remains, however improbable, must be the truth."[1]

Going beyond this, a further desirable prospect is that of an inquiry procedure that is self-corrective. Here, question resolution is addressed by a process that is able not only to detect an error when made but also to produce an alternative that both has promise as an alternative and at least partially rectifies the error at issue. The further our inquiry procedure achieves question resolution, the more suitable it is for its intended work. Nature may or may not abhor a vacuum, but the human mind certainly does. We need to resolve our questions and are so constituted that having a wrong answer may well be preferable to us than having none at all, the prospect of misinformation often being more acceptable than ignorance. And it is here—in relation to our irrepressible quest for information—that error makes its way upon the scene as the great spoiler of the cognitive enterprise.

How do errors come about? What are their sources or causes? There is no prospect of a complete inventory here. The roadways to error are too numerous to admit of anything like a comprehensive listing. The best we can do is to give a handful of prominent examples with regard to cognitive error: inattention, misjudgment, confusion and conflation, miscalculation, under- and overestimation, leaping to conclusions. Correspondingly, error reduction can take many forms: concentration of effort, double checking, proofreading, getting second opinions. There is also the issue of *damage control*—of measures we can take to mitigate the consequences of errors if and when they occur despite our best efforts at minimizing them.

Scepticism is the philosophical doctrine that maintains the infeasibility of attaining knowledge. It takes many forms: there are more versions of scepticism than one can shake a stick at, and no two philosophers have viewed the doctrine in just the same way.[2] However, it revolves generally around variations on the thesis that when we claim to know some particular fact *p*,

> we claim more than is really warranted by the information actually at our disposal (*insufficiency* scepticism), and accordingly, . . .

> we may well be wrong about it (*fallibilistic* scepticism), and therefore should be prepared for the eventuality that, . . .

> we are (always and invariably) going to be wrong about it so that authentic knowledge is simply unattainable (*radical* scepticism).

Radical or (Pyrrhonean) scepticism sees our claims to knowledge as systematically and comprehensively unjustified. A more modest scepticism sees them as being in general defeasible and potentially

error-prone. Such milder scepticism rests on a pretty firm foundation. For not only is "our knowledge" *incomplete,* but we have little alternative to regarding it as presumptively *incorrect and corrigible.* Evi-
dence-in-hand is necessarily limited and finitistic, while our claims to
objective factual knowledge always incorporate elements of nomic
universality. And this enjoins us to recognize a possible "evidential
gap" between our evidence and the asserted content of the objective
factual claims about the real world that we base upon it.

The fallibility of much of our factual knowledge of the world is
exhibited rather than refuted by a consideration of scientific knowledge. For the status of our knowledge as merely *purported* knowledge
is nowhere clearer than with science. Our scientific "knowledge" is
by no means as secure and absolute as is generally pretended. After
all, there is every reason to think that where scientific knowledge is
concerned further knowledge does not just supplement but generally corrects our knowledge-in-hand, so that the incompleteness of
our information implies its presumptive incorrectness as well.

If there is any one thing we can learn from the history of science,
it is that the science of one day is looked upon by the next as naive,
deficient, and somehow wrong from the vantage point of the wisdom of hindsight. The clearest induction from the history of science
is that science is always mistaken—that at *every* stage of its development its practitioners, looking backward with the vision of hindsight, view the work of their predecessors as seriously misinformed
and mistaken in very fundamental respects. We must acknowledge
an *epistemological Copernicanism* that rejects the egocentric claim that
we ourselves occupy a pivotal position in the epistemic dispensation
and recognizes that there is nothing inherently sacrosanct about our
own present cognitive posture vis-à-vis that of other, later historical
junctures. A kind of intellectual humility is called for—a self-abnega-
tory diffidence that abstains from the hubris of pretensions to cognitive finality or centrality. The original Copernican revolution made

the point that there is nothing *ontologically* privileged about our own position in space. The doctrine now at issue effectively holds that there is nothing *cognitively* privileged about our own position in time. It urges that *there is nothing epistemically privileged about the present—any* present, our own prominently included. Such a perspective indicates not only the incompleteness of "our knowledge" but its presumptive incorrectness as well. All this brings much grist to the sceptic's mill. What is the sensible way to deal with it?

SCEPTICISM AND ERROR AVOIDANCE

To be sure, agnosticism is a sure-fire safeguard against errors of commission in cognitive matters. If you accept nothing, then you accept no falsehoods. All ventures in claiming knowledge about reality carry some risk of cognitive error in their wake: it is an unavoidable companion of the enhancement of knowledge. And so we have it that "to err is human."

A less drastic way of insuring against error is to "hedge one's bets" by vagueness. "How old was George Washington when he died?" If I answer "seventy years," my response is at risk, but distinctly less so if I answer "around seventy," and less yet if I say "over sixty." Increased security can always be purchased for our estimates at the price of decreased precision. We estimate the height of a tree at around twenty-five feet. We are *quite sure* that the tree is twenty-five feet high, give or take five feet. We are *virtually certain* that its height is twenty-five give or take ten feet. But we are *completely and absolutely sure* that its height is between one inch and one hundred yards. Of this we are "completely sure" in the sense that we are "absolutely certain," "certain beyond the shadow of a doubt," "as certain as we can be of anything in the world," "so sure that we would be willing to stake our life on it," and the like. For any sort of estimate whatsoever, there is always a characteristic trade-off between, on the one hand, the evidential *security* or *reliability* of the estimate (as determinable on the basis of its probability or degree of acceptability), and, on the other hand, its contentual *definiteness* (exactness, detail, precision). A situation of the sort depicted by the concave curve of figure 3.1 obtains, illustrating how these desiderata are at loggerheads with one another. On this basis, vagueness is an effective instrument for error avoidance; and the less definitely informative one's response to a question is, the better one's chances are of averting error. Thus, as Aristotle noted, we cannot err in viewing an object of thought, whatever it be, as *something* but only in being of this or that particular sort.[3] Only insofar as our thought becomes definite and content-laden can it manage to err. Unfortunately, however, this safety is gained at the cost of informativeness, a circumstance that indicates that error-avoidance is not a be-all and end-all in cognition, since cognitive interests are also at stake. The resulting situation can be depicted as in figure 3.2, which renders it graphically manifest that truth and error avoidance are not everything in epistemology. Informativeness also counts. After all, a true statement does not necessarily describe how things stand in the world. When I say that yon tree (which in fact stands at sixty feet) is "over six feet high," I say something as true as can be but do not go very far toward describing the tree.

As this situation indicates, averting error is not enough. After all, resolutions that succumb to imprecision, vagueness, indefiniteness, and the like, need not be erroneous yet are apt to be unhelpful and uninformative. Accordingly, averting error by vague and insufficient answers to our questions does not offer a very satisfactory route to knowledge. To realize one does not make pancakes from sand, from mercury, from butterfly wings, and so on is certainly to have a great many correct beliefs about the matter. But all *such* error avoidance does not bring one much closer to knowing how pancakes are actually made. The aims of inquiry are not necessarily furthered by the elimination of cognitive errors of commission. For if in eliminat-

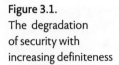

Figure 3.1.
The degradation
of security with
increasing definiteness

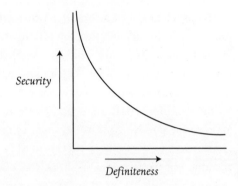

Figure 3.2.
The
information/error
relation

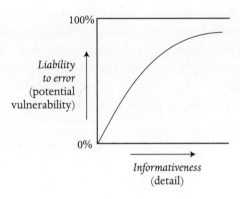

ing such an error, we simply leave behind a blank, and for a wrong answer, substitute no answer at all, we have simply managed to exchange an error of commission for one of omission.

OMISSION AND COMMISSION IN COGNITION

Being mistaken is unquestionably a negativity. When we accept something false, we have failed in our endeavors to get a clear view of things, to answer our questions correctly. And moreover, mistakes tend to ramify, to infect environing issues. If I (correctly) realize that p logically entails q but incorrectly believe not-q, then I am constrained to accept not-p, which may well be quite wrong. Error is fertile of further error. So quite apart from practical matters (suffering painful practical consequences when things go wrong), there are also the purely cognitive penalties of mistakes—entrapment in an incorrect view of things. All this must be granted and taken into account. But the fact remains that errors of commission are not the only sort of misfortune there is.[4] Ignorance, lack of information, cognitive disconnection from the world's course of things—in short, errors of omission—are also negativities of substantial proportions. This too is something we must work into our reckoning. For as figure 3.3 illustrates, errors of omission are the price of averting errors of commission, with errors of one kind balancing off those of another.

In claiming that his position wins out because it makes the fewest

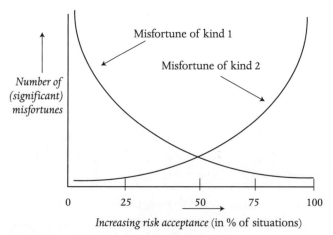

Figure 3.3. Risk acceptance and misfortunes

mistakes, the sceptic uses a fallacious system of scoring, for while he indeed makes the fewest errors of one kind, he does this at the cost of proliferating those of another. Once we look on this matter of error realistically, the sceptic's vaunted advantage vanishes. The sceptic is simply a risk avoider, who is prepared to take no risks and who stubbornly insists on minimizing errors of the second kind alone, heedless of the errors of the first kind into which he falls at every opportunity.

Ultimately, we face a question of value trade-offs. Are we prepared to run a greater risk of mistakes to secure the potential benefit of an enlarged understanding? In the end, the matter is one of priorities— of safety as against information, of ontological economy as against cognitive advantage, of an epistemological risk aversion as against the impetus to understanding. The pivotal issue is one of values and priorities, weighing the negativity of ignorance and incomprehension against the risk of mistakes and misinformation.

The sceptic succeeds splendidly in averting misfortunes of the second kind. He makes no errors of commission; by accepting nothing, he accepts nothing false. But, of course, he loses out on the opportunity to obtain any sort of information. The sceptic thus errs on the side of safety, even as the syncretist errs on that of gullibility. The sensible course is clearly that of a prudent calculation of risks.

The rational person seeks not only to minimize the occurrence of error but also to minimize the adverse consequences of error should it occur notwithstanding this effort. However, such measures are seldom cost free. Misprint-reducing proofreading takes time and effort, warning signals at railway crossings cost money. Such measures only diminish error but do not eliminate it because of its inherence in the chance and chaos that rule the world. Errors are always out there waiting to be made (*"Die Fehler sind ja da um gemacht zu werden,"* my father's drill sergeant told him in 1914). Eliminating error, like creating a vacuum, becomes exponentially more difficult the nearer we approach ever unattainable perfection. The reduction of error is a matter of diminishing returns that is bound to become impracticable at some point.

The crucial fact is that inquiry, like virtually all other human endeavors, is not a cost-free enterprise. The process of getting plausible answers to our questions involves costs and risks. Whether these costs and risks are worth incurring depends on our valuation of the potential benefit to be gained. And unlike the committed sceptic, most of us deem the value of information about the world we live in to be a benefit of immense value, something well worth substantial risks.

RATIONALITY AND THE RISK OF ERROR

Rationality is closely connected to error avoidance. However, a rational cognitive agent need not be someone who commits no errors—this status being unachievable in principle for the finite beings that we are. Rather, it is someone who endeavors to employ those methods, procedures, and processes that yield the minimum of error, the best and most overall, omission included, so as to achieve a favorable balance of truth over ignorance and falsehood in matters of belief and successes over failure and frustration in matters of action.

The reality of it is that *Homo sapiens* has evolved within nature to fill the ecological niche of an intelligent being. The demand for understanding, for a cognitive accommodation to one's environment, for "knowing one's way about" is one of the most fundamental requirements of the human condition. Humans are *Homo quaerens*. We have questions and want (nay, *need*) answers. The need for information, for cognitive orientation in our environment, is as pressing a human need as that for food itself. We are rational animals and must feed our minds even as we must feed our bodies. In pursuing information, as in pursuing food, we have to settle for the best we can get at the time. We have questions and need answers, the best answers we can get here and now, regardless of their imperfections.

The need for knowledge is part and parcel of our human condition. A deep-rooted demand for information and understanding presses in upon us, and we have little choice but to satisfy it. Once the ball is set rolling, it keeps on under its own momentum—far beyond the limits of strictly practical necessity. The great Norwegian polar explorer Fridtjof Nansen put it well. What drives men to the polar regions, he said, is

> the power of the unknown over the human spirit. As ideas
> have cleared with the ages, so has this power extended its
> might, and driven Man willy-nilly onwards along the path
> of progress. It drives us in to Nature's hidden powers and
> secrets, down to the immeasurably little world of the micro-
> scopic, and out into the unprobed expanses of the Universe.
> . . . It gives us no peace until we know this planet on which
> we live, from the greatest depth of the ocean to the high-
> est layers of the atmosphere. This Power runs like a strand
> through the whole history of polar exploration. In spite of
> all declarations of possible profit in one way or another, it
> was that which, in our hearts, has always driven us back
> there again, despite all setbacks and suffering.[5]

The discomfort of unknowing is a natural component of human sensibility. To be ignorant of what goes on about us is almost physically painful for us—no doubt because it is so dangerous from an evolutionary point of view. As William James observed, "The utility of this emotional effect of [security of] expectation is perfectly obvious. 'Natural selection,' in fact, was bound to bring it about sooner or later. It is of the utmost practical importance to an animal that he should have prevision of the qualities of the objects that surround him."

It is a situational imperative for us humans to acquire information about the world. We have questions and we need answers. *Homo sapiens* is a creature that must, by his very nature, feel cognitively at home in the world. Relief from ignorance, puzzlement, and cognitive dissonance is one of cognition's most important benefits. These benefits are both positive (pleasures of understanding) and negative (reducing intellectual discomfort through the removal of unknowing and ignorance and the diminution of cognitive dissonance). The basic human urge to make sense of things is a characteristic aspect of our makeup—we cannot live a satisfactory life in an environment we do not understand. For us, cognitive orientation is itself a practical need: cognitive disorientation is actually stressful and distressing.

Philosophical sceptics often set up some abstract standard of absolutistic certainty and then try to show that no knowledge claims in a certain area (sense, memory, scientific theory, and the like) can possibly meet the conditions of this standard. From this circumstance, the impossibility of such a category of "knowledge" is accordingly inferred. But what follows is rather the inappropriateness or incorrectness of the standard at issue. If the vaunted standard is such that knowledge claims cannot possibly meet it, the moral is not "too bad for knowledge claims," but "too bad for the standard." Any position that precludes in principle the possibility of valid knowledge claims thereby effectively manifests its own unacceptability.

Charles Sanders Peirce never tired of maintaining that inquiry only has a point if we accept from the outset that there is some prospect that it may terminate in a satisfactory answer to our questions. He indicated the appropriate stance with trenchant cogency: "The first question, then, which I have to ask is: Supposing such a thing to be true, what is the kind of proof which I ought to demand to satisfy me of its truth?"[6] A general epistemic policy that would as a matter of principle make it impossible for us to discover *something that is* ex hypothesi *the case* is clearly irrational. And the sceptical proscription of all acceptance is obviously such a policy—one that abrogates the project of inquiry at the very outset, without according it the benefit of a fair trial. A presumption in favor of rationality, cognitive rationality included, is rationally inescapable. It could, to be sure, eventuate at the end of the day that satisfactory knowledge of physical reality is unachievable. But until the end of the proverbial day arrives, we can and should proceed on the idea that this possibility is not a prospect. "Never bar the path of inquiry," Peirce rightly insisted. And radical scepticism's fatal flaw is that it aborts inquiry at the start.

Reason's commitment to the cognitive enterprise of inquiry is absolute and establishes an insatiable demand for extending and deepening the range of our information. As Aristotle was wont to observe, "Man by nature desires to know." In denying the prospect of any sort of rational warrant, however tentative, the all-out sceptic embarks upon a self-imposed exile from the community of communicators, seeing that the communicative use of language is predicated on conceding the warranting presuppositions of language use. To enter into a discussion at all, one must acquiesce in the underlying rules of meaning and information-transmission that make discussion in general possible. But, if *nothing* can appropriately be accepted, then no rules can be established, and thus no statements made, since meaningful discourse requires a commonality of concurrence in the informative conventions.

Safety engineering is the enterprise of error management. Its definitive aims are two: reducing the chance of an occurrence of error and reducing the negative consequences of error should it occur. Requiring a second opinion before taking a potentially risky step illustrates the former process; arranging for automatic "fail-safe" shutdown as a dangerous condition nears illustrates the second. And so the salient lesson of the pervasiveness of error in human affairs is not a nihilistic scepticism but the need for safety engineering. Such safety engineering with its safeguards against unforeseeable and perhaps even unavoidable errors is typical of the rationality's sensibly safety-mindedness in the wake of acknowledging the unavoidability of error.

THE POVERTY OF SCEPTICISM

From such a standpoint, it becomes clear that scepticism purchases the avoidance of mistakes at an unacceptable price. After all, no method of inquiry, no cognitive process or procedure that we can operate in this imperfect world, can be altogether failure free and totally secure against error of every description. Any workable screening process will let some goats in among the sheep. With our cognitive mechanisms, as with machines of any sort, perfection is unattainable; the prospect of malfunction can never be eliminated, at least not at any acceptable price. Of course, we could always add more elaborate safeguarding devices. (We could make automobiles so laden with safety devices that they would become as large, expensive, and cumbersome as busses.) But that defeats the balance of our purposes. A further series of checks and balances prolonging our inquiries by a week (or a decade) might avert certain mistakes. But for each mistake avoided, we would lose much information. Safety engineering in inquiry is like safety engineering in life. There must be proper balance between costs and benefits. If accident avoidance were all that mattered, we could take our mechanical technology back to the Stone Age and our cognitive technology as well.

The sceptic's insistence on safety at any price is simply unrealistic, if only on the essentially economic basis of a sensible balance of costs and benefits. Since the days of the Academic Sceptics of classical antiquity, various philosophers have addressed our present question—Why accept anything at all?—by taking the line that man is a rational animal. As an animal, he must act, since his very survival depends upon action. But as a rational being, he cannot act availingly save insofar as his actions are guided by his beliefs, by what he accepts. This argument has been revived in modern times by a succession of pragmatically minded thinkers, from David Hume to William James. And if belief's guidance of action were indeed all there were to it, this perspective would perhaps do. The mitigated sceptics of the Middle Academy were possibly quite right in thinking that we do not need certain knowledge because plausible belief *(to pithanon)* is often enough to meet our needs. But it unfortunately will not serve when we want actual answers to our questions. If it is *information* we want—and, indeed, need to rest content as the sorts of inquiring beings we are—then we have to go further. Risk of error is so worth running because it is unavoidable in the context of the cognitive project of rational inquiry. Here, as elsewhere, the situation is simply one of nothing ventured, nothing gained.

In the final analysis, the sceptic thus runs afoul of the demands of that very rationality in whose name he so high-mindedly claims to speak. Rationality, after all, is not a matter of *logic* alone—of commitment to the logical principles of consistency (that is, not to accept what contradicts accepted premisses) and completeness (that is, to accept what is entailed by accepted premisses), which are, after all, purely hypothetical in nature ("If you accept . . . , then——"). It is not just a *hypothetical* issue of making proper inferences from premisses but also encompasses the *categorical* issue of giving their proper evidential weight to the premisses themselves.

The sceptic is thus not embarked on a *defense* of reason but on a self-imposed *exile* from the enterprise of cogent discussion and the community of rational inquirers. And at this juncture he is no longer left in possession of the high ground. In refusing to give to the standard evidential considerations the presumptive and *prima facie* weight that is their established value on the market of rational interchange, the sceptic, rather than being the defender of rigid reason, is in fact profoundly irrational. The sceptic *seemingly* moves within the orbit of rationality. But by his refusal to acknowledge the ordinary probative rules of plausibility, presumption, evidence, and so on, he effectively opts out of the rational enterprise of our standard practice in the interests of what can count as knowledge according to some inappropriately hyperbolic standard.

There is, of course, nothing whatsoever desirable about error in itself. But, nevertheless, in the larger scheme of things something positive can be said on its behalf. For, in a way, error is a blessing in disguise; it is the price to be paid for the realization of a larger good. Knowledge progresses via error: we are, or should be, engaged in an ongoing process of learning from our mistakes. And on the side of praxis it is a pervasive reality that the path to more adequate performances is paved with less adequate ones. For finite beings like ourselves, mistakes are integral to and inseparable from the learning process. And so it is sensible to regard error not as an unqualified negativity but, rather, given the inexorable realities, as constituting the inseparable dark side of positivity.

Take cognitive error in particular. We humans live and act under the guidance of information: we do what we do on the basis of what we believe. But here the crucial distinction between belief and knowledge comes into play. To live our lives under the aegis of thought we have to be able to answer questions and resolve issues that go beyond what we are actually able to ascertain securely. To cope in this world, a creature that acts on the basis of thought needs to extend its beliefs beyond the range of yet secured knowledge. Its action requires question resolutions, and these in turn force its beliefs beyond the secure confines of knowledge. For such a creature cognitive risk is unavoidable. And this means that in theory and in practice alike, liability to error accompanies the benefit of being intelligent agents rather than reflex-governed automata; it is simply a part of the price we unavoidably pay for the realization of a larger good.

Error and Oversimplification

OVERSIMPLIFICATION

To save time, effort, or breath we often deliberately simplify matters, realizing full well that some aspect or feature of reality is being omitted from view. But this does not worry us because we have good and sufficient reason to believe that the overlooked item, whatever it is, simply does not matter for present purposes. However, this sort of thing is simplification and not oversimplification. When oversimplification occurs, then it transpires, more or less by definition, that we are going too far with simplification—that what is being lost sight of is something that does indeed matter, because simplification has been carried to the point where it makes a real difference and involves a real loss.

Oversimplification always involves errors of omission. It occurs whenever someone leaves out of account features of an item that bear upon a correct understanding of its nature. For example, to say that Rome declined because its elite was enervated by lead poisoning from the pipes of its water supply oversimplifies the issue by fixing on one single causal factor to the exclusion of many others. It is inevitable for overly simple thought about anything to be incomplete, because that's exactly what oversimplification is—the omission of significant detail through a failure to take note of factors that are germane to the matters at hand, thereby resulting in a failure to understand the reality of things. Whenever we unwittingly oversimplify matters, we have a blind spot where some facet of reality is concealed from our view.

Oversimplification occurs when simplification is carried to an extent that is counterproductive in relation to the aims of the enterprise at hand. It consists in a failure to provide not *all* detail whatsoever (which is unavoidable) but all issue-pertinent detail. It can occur only in a procedural or functional context where one is concerned with *doing* something, even if this doing is only a matter of securing information to answer our questions about some matter. It is exactly this procedural or factual context that determines and defines the relevancy range for the matters at issue. In this regard it seems plausible and useful to grade relevancy on a scale from zero to ten, somewhat in line with the following array of adverbs:

Crucially (10)

Importantly/majorly (8)

Significantly/substantially (6)

Minimally/marginally (4)

Irrelevantly/immaterially (2)

Wholly beside the point (0)

Oversimplification thus consists in the omission of detail in a way that is misleading in creating or inviting a wrong impression in some *significant*—that is, issue-relevant—regard. In practice the line between beneficial simplification and harmful oversimplification is not easy to draw. Often as not, it can only be discerned with the wisdom of hindsight. For whether that loss of detail has negative consequences and repercussions is generally not clear until after a good many returns are in. And of course it is going to be highly context dependent. For the neglect of certain details can matter crucially in one context and yet be irrelevant in another. It seems not so much an oversimplification as a truism to say, "a dollar bill is just that—a dollar bill; it matters not whether it is crisp or crumpled." And that is true enough where paying the cashier is concerned. But in dealing with the oversensitive parking lot machine that insists upon new, crisp bills, the status of that bill may make a big difference.

Why do we ever oversimplify? Why not just go ahead and take those ignored complications into account? The answer is that in the circumstances we simply do not know how to. The situation is akin to that of the paradox of the preface. Recall that the author writes: "I want to thank X, Y, and Z for their help with the material in the book. I apologize to the reader for the remaining errors, which are entirely mine." One is, of course, tempted to object: "Why apologize for those errors? Why not simply correct them?" But, alas, our author cannot *identify* his errors. *That* there are errors, he realizes; what they are, he does not. The situation with oversimplification is much the same. All too often we realize *that* we oversimplify, what we do not know is *where* we oversimplify. This is, in general, something that we can discern only within the wisdom of hindsight.

Oversimplification leads to error not just in matters of belief but in matters of action as well. For, here, oversimplification generally engenders inefficiency. Consider, for example, the following situation:

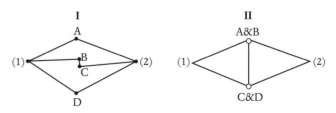

Suppose that in fact points 1 and 2 are linked by the road network sketched in I. Suppose further, though, that one's map of the system is oversimplified by a failure of discrimination that amalgamates points *A* and *B* and also points *C* and *D* so that the map looks like the situation in II. Clearly, such an oversimplification is going to invite a loss in terms of transit efficiency and thereby engender an incorrect and misleading view of procedural optimalities.

Oversimplification plays a critical role throughout all contexts of information processing—be it in inquiry (information development) or inference (information exploitation) or communication (information transmission). The entire range of information management sees oversimplification entering upon the scene, often with decidedly unhappy results.

WHEN OMISSION LEADS TO COMMISSION

Oversimplification involves loss. The student who never progresses from Lamb's *Tales from Shakespeare* to the works of the bard of Avon himself pays a price, not just in detail of information but in the comprehension of significance. The student who substitutes the Cliff's Notes version for the work itself suffers a comparable impoverishment. To oversimplify a work of literature is to miss much of its very point. Whenever we oversimplify matters by neglecting potentially relevant detail, we succumb to the flaw of *superficiality*. Our understanding of matters then lacks depth and thereby compromises its cogency. But this is not the worst of it. One of the salient aspects of oversimplification lies in the fundamental epistemological fact that errors of omission often carry errors of commission in their wake: that ignorance plunges us into actual mistakes.

Oversimplification is, at bottom, nothing but a neglect (or ignorance) of detail. Its beginnings and origination lie in a lack of detail—in errors of omission. But that is not by any means the end of the matter. For such errors of omission all too readily carry errors of commission in their wake. When confronted with

C C — C C

we conclude that the missing letter is a C instead of an A that may well actually be there. When we fill in gaps and omissions—as we all too generally do—we are likely to slide along the slippery slope of convenience by allowing simplification to lead us into error.

It might seem on first thought that, since oversimplification always roots in errors of omission, it will retain this feature overall and at least spare us from errors of commission. This hopeful expectation is in fact disappointed. If you oversimplify the symbol ~ to - you will not be prepared for the variations you will eventually encounter in reality. Suppose, for example, that the reality of it is this:

(R) | $a\,a\,A$ | $a\,A\,A$ |

And let it be that we "oversimplify" matters by failing to differentiate between a and A, viewing both alike simply as instances of one common α. We then arrive at the following *model* of reality:

(M) | $\alpha\,\alpha\,\alpha$ | $\alpha\,\alpha\,\alpha$ |

Now, on the basis of this we are led straightaway to conclude that, "Both compartments are exactly the same in composition"—a clearly erroneous belief.

Whenever there is a blank in our knowledge, the natural and indeed the sensible thing to do is to fill it in in the most direct, standard, plausible way. We assume that the person we bump into in the street speaks English, so we say, "oops, sorry"—even though this may well prove to be altogether unavailing. We regard the waiter in the restaurant as ours even where it is the brother who bears a family resemblance. We follow the most straightforward and familiar routes up to the point where a "detour" sign appears. We willingly and deliberately adopt the policy of allowing oversimplification to lead us to error time and again because we realize it does so less frequently than the available alternatives.

DOES MORE OVERSIMPLIFICATION HAVE TO MEAN MORE ERROR?

Consider this hopeful idea: *The less the extent of oversimplification, the more probable the correctness of our judgments becomes.* However, this is in fact quite false. Let it be that the reality of it is as shown here:

We could "simplify" this in this way:

And we could carry simplification yet further by going on to this:

However, only this further, additional oversimplification will point us to the (actual) situation reflected in the truth that both branches are exactly alike. A *less* oversimplified model of the situation can very possibly lead our judgment away in key regards. Not only is it the case that mere oversimplification can lead us from truth to falsity; it is also true (and no doubt to some extent regrettable) that in various circumstances further, *additional* oversimplification can lead from falsity back to truth.

SCIENTIFIC PROGRESS AND COGNITIVE COMPLEXITY

Why does oversimplification occur in science? Why is it effectively inevitable here? The answer is that oversimplification is inherent in the very nature of cognitive rationality as it functions in scientific inquiry. Empirical science is a matter of drawing universal conclusions ("theories," as they are usually called) from the perceived facts of observation and experiment. But observation and experimentation are continually enhanced by technological advance in the devices used to monitor and manipulate nature. A web of theory woven about a given manifold of data will not—and effectively cannot—be adequate to the situation that arises after our body of information has become enhanced.

The progress of science proceeds in the wake of ever more elaborate technology for acquiring and processing data. This process increasingly sophisticates the distinctions drawn and increasingly refines the theories employed in providing explanations.[1] We naturally adopt throughout rational inquiry—and, accordingly, throughout natural science—the methodological principle of rational economy to "try the simplest solutions first" and then to make this result do as long as it can. For rationality enjoins us to operate on the basis of Occam's razor—considerations are never to be introduced where they are not required: complexity is never to be posted beyond necessity. Our theories must be minimalistic: they must fit the existing data tightly. This means that as our data are amplified through new observations and experiments the previously prevailing theories will almost invariably become destabilized. Those old theories oversimplified matters: new conditions call for new measures, new data for more complex theories. It lies in the rational economy of sensible inquiry that the history of science is an ongoing litany of oversimple old theories giving way to more sophisticated new ones that correct their oversimplification of the old.

Accordingly, economy and simplicity serve as cardinal directives for inductive reasoning, whose procedure is that of the precept: "Resolve your cognitive problems in the simplest, most economical way that is compatible with a sensible exploitation of the information at your disposal." This means that *historically* the course of inquiry moves in the direction of ever increasing complexity and diminishing oversimplification. The developmental tendency of our intellectual enterprises, natural science among them, is generally in the direction of greater complication and sophistication.

Induction with respect to the history of science itself—a veritable litany of errors of oversimplification—soon undermines our confidence that nature operates in the way we would deem the simpler. On the contrary, the history of science is an endlessly repetitive story of simple theories giving way to more complicated and sophisticated ones. The Greeks had four elements; in the nineteenth century Mendeleev had some sixty; by the 1900s this had gone to eighty, and nowadays we have a vast series of elemental stability states. Aristotle's cosmos had only spheres; Ptolemy's added epicycles; ours has a virtually endless proliferation of complex orbits that only supercomputers can approximate. Greek science was contained on a single shelf of books; that of the Newtonian age required a roomful; ours requires vast storage structures filled not only with books and journals but with photographs, microfilm, CDs, and so on. Of the quantities currently recognized as the fundamental constants of physics, only one was contemplated in Newton's physics: the universal gravitational constant. A second was added in the nineteenth century, Avogadro's constant. The remaining six are all creatures of twentieth-century physics: the speed of light (the velocity of electromagnetic radiation in free space), the elementary charge, the rest mass of an electron, the rest mass of a proton, Planck's constant, and Boltzmann's constant.[2]

It would be naïve, and quite wrong, to think that the course of scientific progress is one of increasing simplicity. The very reverse is the case: scientific progress is a matter of complexification because oversimple theories invariably prove untenable in a complex world. The natural dialectic of scientific inquiry ongoingly impels us into ever deeper levels of sophistication.[3] In this regard our commitment to simplicity and systematicity, though methodologically necessary, is ontologically unavailing. More sophisticated searches invariably engender changes of mind moving in the direction of an ever more complex picture of the world. Our methodological commitment to simplicity should not and does not stand in the way of an ongoing discovery of complexity.

Consider just one example. In the eleventh (1911) edition of the *Encyclopedia Britannica* physics is described as a discipline composed of 9 constituent branches (such as "acoustics" and "electricity and magnetism"), which were themselves partitioned into 20 further specialties (like "thermo-electricity of celestial mechanics"). The fifteenth (1974) edition divides physics into 12 branches whose subfields are, seemingly, too numerous for listing. (However the fourteenth, 1960, edition carried a special article titled "Physics, Articles on," which surveyed more than 130 special topics in the field.) When in 1954 the National Science Foundation launched its inventory of physical specialties with the National Register of Scientific and Technical Personnel, it divided physics into 12 areas with 90 specialties. By 1970 these figures had increased to 16 and 210, respectively. And the process continues unabated to the point where people are increasingly reluctant to embark on this classifying project at all.

An inherent impetus toward greater complexity pervades the entire realm of human creative effort. We find it in art, in technology, and certainly in the cognitive domain.[4] In science the salient lesson is that we continually oversimplify.

At this point we encounter a conflict of ideas that is best described eponymously. For, on the one hand, there stands J. M. Keynes' *principle of limited variety,* which has it that nature is finitely complex and that reality can be comprehensively characterized in a finite number of natural descriptive kinds. And, on the other hand, there stands G. W. Leibniz's *principle of infinite detail* which envisions an infinitely complex nature whose endless variation of detail is such that every ultimate unit of existence is effectively a species unto itself. This would mean that any and every human effort at characterizing reality and its modus operandi is destined to be an oversimplification. Clearly, there is a choice between these two positions, but equally clearly it is the more highly differentiated Leibnizian stance with its insistence on the inevitability of oversimplification that has the aura of greater plausibility.

CONFUSION, CONFLATION, AND THEIR CONSEQUENCES

To this point we have addressed the what, where, and why of oversimplification. Let us now consider what it leaves in its wake—specifically, what the implications are of the fact that the science we have in hand oversimplifies the reality of things. Let us begin by going back to basics. Confusion and conflation are two prime modes of oversimplification. The key ideas at issue here are to be understood as follows:

X confuses items *x* and *y* over the question-manifold *Q* iff in answering the questions within this manifold *X* fails to distinguish between *x* and *y*.

X conflates items *x* and *y* over the question-manifold *Q* iff in answering the question within the manifold *X* sees both *x* and *y* as one selfsame *z*.

This cognitive myopia, as noted earlier, now takes two forms:

Mild version: An *occasional confusion* between two distinct sorts of items , as for example when there is an occasional mix-up in construing *h* as *k*, or conversely.

Strong version: A *systemic conflation*, as, for example, when both *h* and *k* appear simply as a fuzzy and indistinguishable blurred complex.

For the sake of illustration, consider someone whose visual myopia is such that she is unable to tell 5 and 6 apart. As a result of such an inability, the individual may well, through *conflation,*

envision 56 as ✳✳

Or, again, the individual may, through *confusion,*

envision 56 as 66

Such forms of cognitive myopia have very different ramifications for our grasp of the world's lawful comportment. Suppose that we are in reality dealing with the perfectly regular series

$R: 6\,5\,6\,5\,6\,5\,6\,5\,6\,5\ldots,$

but owing to the occasional confusion arising from a mild cognitive myopia, we may actually "see" this (whether by observing or conceptualizing) as

$M: 6\ 5\ 5\ 5\ 6\ 5\ 5\ 5\ 6\ 5 \ldots$

But observe that our inability to distinguish has here effectively transmuted a lawful regularity into a random disorder. It is then clear (via "Mill's methods of agreement and difference") that there is no causal correlation between R and M. The supposition of (mild) myopia thus induces a drastic disconnection between the two levels of consideration at issue, with the lawful order of R giving way to lawlessness in regard to its model M. Thus even so crude an example suffices to show that lawful order can unravel and be destroyed by the confusion engendered by an occasional inability to discern differences. This relatively rudimentary observation has far-reaching implications. Specifically, it means that even if the world is possessed of a highly lawful order, this feature of reality may well fail to be captured in even a mildly myopic representation of it. This, in turn, means that, given myopia, the world view presented in our world-modeling may well be no more than loosely coupled to the underlying reality of things thanks to the oversimplification that is almost inevitably involved.

MORE EXAMPLES

Let the actually real situation be:

FFG	FG
FG	FFG

Suppose our limited oversimplifying perspective gives us a look at only two adjacent components. We would then have at our disposal the following two views of the situation:

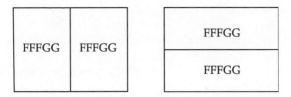

That conjectural restriction of the situation will then lead us, likely as not, to conjecture the simplest, most uniform and symmetric resolution so as to arrive at the following model of the reality at hand:

FFF	GG
GG	FFF

Here our conjectural reasoning will lead to some correct results as "uniformity along diagonals" as well as the erroneous "all compartments are homogeneous." Cognitive myopia need not be harmful; but it can be.

Suppose a system consisting of three types of objects A, B, and C, with an initial state of two items of type A and one each of types B and C. Let it be that this system develops through successive stages or phases that see these types of objects formed according to the following rules:

$A \rightarrow B$

$B \rightarrow C$

$C \rightarrow A$

The result in point of their classification will be as the following series:

	(1)	(2)	(3)	(4)	$\longrightarrow$
A	2	1	1		
B	1	2	1		} cyclic repetiton
C	1	1	2		

But now suppose that owing to oversimplification *A*s and *B*s are not distinguished but seen as one uniform type, $A^\star$. We then have

	(1)	(2)	(3)	(4)	$\longrightarrow$
$A^\star$	3	3	2		
C	1	1	2		} cyclic repetiton

Now every third period, one-third of the earlier $A^\star$s (one cannot say which third!) mysteriously migrates to the *C*s with half of the *C*s (again, no saying which) switching to $A^\star$s in the succeeding period. What is in actuality a simple and deterministic situation is transmuted through oversimplification into an indeterministic mysterium whose modus operandi is ruled by stochastic variation. However, there is also the prospect of a severe cognitive myopia that results in a *systemic conflation* of reality in the setting of its conceptualization. For the sake of illustration, let it thus be that the reality that confronts us has the following random structure:

6 5 5 6 6 6 5 5 5 6 5 5 6 6 5 . . .

But let it also be that in representing this reality in our observations and/or conceptualization our vision of the matter is so myopic that we cannot readily distinguish between 5 and 6: both simply look like a blurring (5-or-6) to us. Then the above chaotic series is representatively transmitted into the elegant uniformity of the following series:

$(5\text{-or-}6)(5\text{-or-}6)(5\text{-or-}6)(5\text{-or-}6)\ldots$

Where reality is in fact random and discordant, its representation in our cognitive field of vision is the quintessence of lawful elegance. For under the conditions at issue, we will have it that a world whose physical comportment is in certain respects random and lawless may well be seen by its cognitively myopic observers as having a phenomenology that is deterministically lawful.

As these considerations indicate, oversimplification can easily distort our view of the lawful structure of the world. It can either lead to a nomic deficit that reflects the loss of various actual laws or to a nomic surfeit that gives the illusion of loss when there is none. By its very nature as a process of cognitive omission, oversimplification conceals certain actual regularities from our view. Moreover, insofar as it makes matters appear more uniform than they actually are, it is virtually bound to lead to spurious regularities. The point is that there are not only optical illusions of the bodily visions but also comparable cognitive illusions where we exercise our mental vision to grasp the ways of the world. Our oversimplified models of reality distort our view of its modes of operation in ways that not only block various lawful regularities from our view but also project spacious regularities onto the screen of mind. We have no alternative to deeming science-as-we-have-it to afford an oversimplified model of reality. Consequently, we have no alternative to deeming it to be involved in the same shortcomings that beset oversimplification in general.

ULTIMATE LESSONS

While the oversimplification at issue with conflation and confusion differ significantly, they both conspire to raise the prospect of a significant decoupling between the order of reality *(R)* and our cognitive modeling *(M)* of it—between the lawful order of nature *(N)* and its representation in the law-manifold encapsulated in the science of the day *(S)*. We would, ideally, love to have it that reality and our view of it are duly aligned, so that $M = R$ and $S = N$. But in view of the effectively inevitable presence of cognitive myopia we can neither claim nor expect this.

Oversimplification has significant consequences, and we have little alternative but to accept (1) that science as we actually have it affords us with an oversimplified model of Reality, and (2) that what holds for oversimplification in general will apply in this particular case as well. Taken together, what this means is that one must adopt a fallibilism that accepts that our science is involved, not merely with errors of omission but with errors of commission as well—that nature's lawful modus operandi is not adequately and accurately depicted through the resources of science as we have it. We have to be fallibilistic and realistic about it. We do and must expect that the natural science of the day, any day, will not only be incomplete in its characterization of reality but, in some respects, incorrect as well. No doubt science affords our best-available estimates regarding the ways of the world. But as regards the truth about Reality, we cannot but accept that science does not give us the whole of it nor even nothing but. Here, as elsewhere, the prospect of error—alike of omission and commission—is uneliminable for finite intelligences who operate under conditions of imperfect information.

A CODA ON MYOPIA AND RANDOMNESS

Observe that, as a consequence of this oversimplification, even an elegant physical order (ϕ) may well be reflected confusedly at the cognitive/psychological level (ψ)—and in such a way that its representation involves a substantially random and disordered phenomenology at the cognitive/psychological level in the realm of thought. With cognitive myopia our modality of reality may well become estranged from the actualities. And given that rational agents will themselves act within nature on the basis of their *understanding* of things, it will transpire that even in an otherwise lawful and deterministic world this order will break down once imperfectly intelligent agents evolve and cognitive myopia deconstructs the world's lawful order. Thus let it be in particular that such an agent is programmed to respond according to the following *rule of behavior* (be it internally or externally mandated):

Wherever you see a 5, do A but otherwise do not.

But now reconsider our prior hypothetical example of 5-6 confusion. We will then have it that the agent will produce the following behavior sequence:

$$A - A\,A\,A - A - \ldots$$

Our myopic agent has thus inserted into physical reality what is (via our hypotheses) an essentially random sequence that transmutes an otherwise lawful and deterministic world into one that is (in at least one respect) lawless and random—even at the level of its physical comportment. Myopic perception at the level of appearance has introduced a randomness-productive disconnection between the actual physical phenomenology and the realm of psychic operations.

✕ 5 ✕

Error and Morality

MORAL ERROR

Moral error pivots on intention, and moral reprehensibility on malevolence. Moral error is not a particularly popular topic nowadays. But the fact remains that no discussion of error can be deemed adequate that leaves sin entirely out of the account. For in matters of practice, error consists in doing things wrong, and sin is, after all, one of the most notable sorts of wrongdoing there is.

With legal and moral culpability alike, error is an important issue. For one thing, agents acting in good faith in light of a circumstantially plausible error for which they are nowise responsible are free of moral (albeit, not always legal) culpability. The borrower who by mistake unwittingly returns a borrowed item to the owner's irresponsible identical twin is innocent of moral, albeit, not necessarily legal, culpability, as is the nurse who unknowingly administers as a medicament a poison that was malevolently substituted in its place. In such cases error there applies the maxim of Roman law that consent and intent are negated by error *(non videntur, qui errant, consentire)*.

To be sure, if carried through to its logical conclusion, this principle could virtually annihilate commercial transaction. In consequence a practice made under an erroneous (albeit, not fraudulently engendered) impression holds good, subject to the principle of *caveat emptor*. And the same holds true of other bargains and contents.

The Roman legal principle that an error-based contract is no contract at all holds only when those errors on one party's part are deliberately induced by the other—that is, in cases of fraud. Otherwise, in contracts as in sales, *caveat emptor* applies once more, in view of an indefeasible presumption that, deliberate deceit apart, the buyer intends to purchase what the seller has on offer.[1]

Moral error is a version of practical error, and here, too, error is a matter of counterproductivity. But here it is not a matter of impeding the realization of *chosen* aims and objectives but rather of impeding the realization of that situationally mandated objective of a proper care for the best interests of our fellows. The person who "falls into error" here offends against her real or true interest in the well-being of the human community at large. (To be sure, sins are not created equal in destructiveness—gluttony or envy are one sort of thing and murder and mayhem another.)

But just exactly what valid objects are and what real interest is at stake here? The answer that philosophers have given over the centuries since Plato has focused on seeing ourselves as bearers of worth, of deserving the approbation of those whom we ourselves can, do, and should regard as creditable individuals. On such a view, the loss that is engendered by moral error falls heavily (among whatever other places may be at issue) upon ourselves. For in the end the interests of others that constitute the crux of morality are inextricably interconnected with a due care for one's own interests. In the wake of destruction left by the vandal, the psychopath, the theme is always also the self-inflicted injury of the individual at issue. Moral transgression is self-destructive—in blocking the way to a benign sense of self-worth. A nonnegligible part of the harm that most transgression engenders always falls upon the agent himself.

The tight linkage between practical error and morality is forged by the fact that other people can also suffer the consequences of one's errors. For this reason, one of the most complex issues of moral philosophy is that of one's responsibility to protect others from the adverse consequences of error. Where our own conduct is concerned, this responsibility is transparently clear. But where their own errors are concerned, the situation is murky in the extreme! Parents generally realize this in seeking to tread the difficult line between risks of harm and overprotection that denies children a useful opportunity to learn by their own mistakes. (And where other, unrelated adults are concerned, the situation is even more difficult—as the police called in to intervene in domestic disputes soon come to recognize at potential risk to themselves.)

IS MORAL ERROR EPISTEMIC?

How does moral error differ from epistemic error? Wrongful action that results from a (nonculpably) erroneous understanding of the situation is error all right but not moral error. In its most typical form, moral error is not just a matter of misunderstanding—a failure to get the facts straight—but rather a misjudgment that thinks a certain way of acting to be acceptable that just is not. It consists in being culpably obtuse (or even perverse) rather than merely mistaken.

Do people who commit errors deserve reproach and reprehension, or are they more to be pitied than censured? It all depends on the issue of culpability, which in turn depends on the source or cause of the error. Was it due to inattention, carelessness, reckless disregard of standard safeguards, or some such? Then blame is, indeed, in order. Or was it due to matters lying outside the agent's knowledge and control—to developments he could not be expected to foresee or could not have helped even if he did so? Then that is something else again. Blameworthiness subsists only where the capacity to do otherwise is present, and error is something that we finite and imperfect creatures just cannot avoid. What is reprehensible, then, is not so much falling into error but rather persisting in it despite ample opportunities to get "to know better." It is not error as such but a stubborn, willful, and unthinking persistence in its grasp that is wicked and reprehensible. Only when someone commits an error that they could and should at least have *tried* to prevent do they merit reprehension.

We often speak of erring in the interest of some positive desideratum—for instance, of erring "on the side of caution," "of safety," or "of generosity." Error can be committed in the name of virtue. One can be too trusting, too generous, too helpful. Standardly productive practices can be overdone to the point of counterproductiveness.[2] The error that is (by hypothesis) at issue in such cases is real enough, since an act of wrong-doing or wrong-thinking is at issue. But, of course, in cases of this particular sort the good intentions that underlay the act might diminish the extent of its reprehensibility.

It would serve the interests of theoretical tidiness if erroneous action arose always and only from errors of cognition, if all wrongdoing were just a matter of wrong-thinking, of misinformation. Then cognitive imperfection—foolishness and folly—would do the whole job, and sinfulness and evil in its many forms (perversity, sociopathy, pure nastiness, vandalism, schadenfreude) could be dismissed as a separate force and factor. And in fact much of Greek moral philosophy from Socrates to the Stoics moved in this direction.

The philosophers of ancient Greece confronted the following apory of individually plausible but collectively inconsistent propositions: (1) Man is a rational animal: We frequently do, and ideally always should, do what we do for sound reasons. (2) The only sound reason for an action is that performing it will make us better off. (3) Immoral action will never render us better off. (4) Immoral action is a fact of life: People do often act immorally. Inconsistency prevails here because propositions 1, 2, and 3 hold that immoral action will never occur, thus contradicting proposition 4. Mere logical consistency accordingly requires that one (at least) of these theses be rejected. Greek philosophy ranks the changes of possibility as follows:

> (1)-rejection. (1a) *Irrationalism*: People do not always act rationally: Outright irrationality has a grasp on human affairs. (1b) *Delusionism*: We do what we do for what we *see* as good reasons, but we are frequently mistaken about this.

> (2)-rejection. *Hedonism*: The satisfaction of mere wants, irrespective of whether this actually makes us better off, is a good reason and sufficient for action (the Sophists).

> (3)-rejection. *Immoralism*: Immorality can pay off. People can and do often achieve benefit from wrongdoing (Thrasymachus and political "realists").

> (4)-rejection. *Amoralism*: Morality is an illusion; strictly speaking, there is no such thing as right or wrong (the Cynics).

Plato's dialogue *Theaetetus* traverses the ground of this apory in detail and argues in effect that (1)-rejection is the proper resolution here. For the Platonic Socrates has it that the chain of inconsistency is to be broken via the distinction that while man is indeed a would-be rational being who as such acts for what he sees as good reasons, nevertheless in the event we are often simply mistaken about this. Immorality is indeed real according to (4), and both (2) and (3) are quite correct. But man is only imperfectly rational, and we often act in the *mistaken* belief that an immoral action will render us better off. Accordingly, moral wrongdoing is always rooted in cognitive error, and (1b) represents the appropriate resolution.

With the emergence of Christian theology, such a Platonic view of the world—the moral world in particular—underwent a profound change. For while Christian thought also broke the aforementioned apory's chain of inconsistency by rejecting (1), it took the harsher line of (1a), rejecting Platonic delusionism in favor of an irrationalism that accepted human perversity in the manner of wickedness and sinfulness. Christianity, in sum, saw the failings of human rationality in a bleaker light that grounded wrongdoing in flaws of character rather than failings of intellect. As such a position saw it, wrongdoing, practical error, is not necessarily reducible to theoretical error but is inherent in the very makeup of the human person as a sinful being.

IS EPISTEMIC ERROR IMMORAL?

The idea of viewing belief and cognitive acceptance as also being a mode of action goes back to Duns Scotus and René Descartes, both of whom held that cognitive error is always voluntary. After all, so they reasoned, we always have the option of suspending belief, seeing that the situation we confront here admits the following options:

$$
\left\{
\begin{array}{l}
\text{Suspend} \quad \text{(refrain from commitment)} \\[2ex]
\text{Commit} \left\{
\begin{array}{l}
\text{Positively via acceptance} \\[1ex]
\text{Negatively via rejection}
\end{array}
\right.
\end{array}
\right.
$$

Thus as Descartes in particular saw it, cognitive error, the acceptance of falsehoods, always invokes an element of moral culpability. For given the ubiquitous possibility of suspending belief, the individual who errs in accepting a falsehood generally takes the willful and perverse misstep of staking a cognitive claim where none is justified. In essence, Descartes anticipates the anathema of William Kingdon

Clifford in relation to finite beliefs. However, the thesis that cognitive error is culpable cannot be sustained in the final analysis. For, viewed in a clearer light, suspension too is a mode of issue resolution. Refraining from commitment itself represents a commitment of sorts. An explicit refusal to decide constitutes a mode of decision—and, indeed, one that may in various circumstances fail to afford the optimal and most responsible alternative.

A claim to knowledge undoubtedly calls for an entitlement-to-assent, a "right to be sure." But the entitlement at issue is not a right in the specifically moral sense of the term. For the obligation to be rational is not a *moral* obligation, and lapses from rationality are not *moral* lapses. They do not violate the valid claims of others but involve the frustration of one's own objectives as a member in good standing within the community of rational inquirers. After all, William James' injunction "Achieve truth" is no less cogent than the English philosopher William Kingdon Clifford's "Avoid falsehood." In his classic 1877 essay "The Ethics of Belief" (to which James' even more notorious 1895 essay "The Will to Believe" offered a reply), Clifford maintained his famous thesis that, "It is wrong always, everywhere, and for anyone, to believe anything upon insufficient evidence."[3] Here, Clifford saw the "wrong" at issue as a mode of moral transgression—an irresponsible failing of cognitive conscientiousness that verges on culpable malfeasance in a rational creature.

To be sure, Clifford's dictum must be construed with care. If *wrong* were altered to merely *mistaken,* the thesis would become transformed into an unproblematic platitude. For just that is exactly what we *mean* when speaking of "*insufficient* evidence"—evidence whose employment as a proper basis of credence commits an error of omission. But given this replacement, the thesis would no longer bear the moral overtones that Clifford unquestionably intended it to have, as shown by his talk of "duties" and "guilt" in this connection. Clifford saw a violation of the rules of rational procedure in the cognitive domain as an effectively *ethical* transgression. His discussion thus gave rise to a new project, the "ethics of belief," and some writers even go so far as to push this approach to its logical conclusion by pressing it toward the boundaries that separate the morally reprehensible from the legally criminal.[4] Yet this approach runs into deep difficulties. For in matters of objective fact it is inevitable that the assertive *content* of our claims outstrips information we can ever gather by way of supportive *evidence* for them. The prospect of error is simply unavoidable here, and there is nothing irrational—let alone *wrong*—about accepting this risk. Quite to the contrary: "A rule of thinking which would absolutely prevent me from acknowledging certain kinds of truth, if those kinds of truth were really there, would be an irrational rule."[5] Only by being willing to run in the race do we stand a chance, however slim, of winning it: "Nothing ventured, nothing gained." Accepting the risk of error is not a sin but rather the most fundamental requisite of the cognitive life.[6]

To insist always and everywhere on conclusive, ironclad evidence is to bay at the moon. After all, even inconclusive evidence is still *evidence*. As such, it may fall short of a foolproof guarantee, but acceptance can be in order even where the prospect of error cannot be categorically precluded. Yet it is hardly sensible to invoke moral wrongdoing here. In running epistemic risks we surely commit no specifically *ethical* or *moral* violation. The issue is one of self-deprivation rather than of moral turpitude—of prudential losses rather than ethical transgressions.

In light of such considerations, Clifford's ethico-moral approach to belief seems very questionable. The goals relevantly operative in the cognitive sphere relate not to our moral ends but to the prudential means involved in the proper management of rational inquiry, exposition, discussion, and argumentation. The sanctions of erroneous cognition are not those of *morality* but of interest-geared rationality—of prudential rather than ethical standards. To be sure, even cognitive errors can deserve reproach—especially so when due to such failings and deficiencies as inattention, carelessness, or the like. But the failings at issue are not inherently moral but prudential. The rules of ethics and morality are correlative with the purpose of avoiding damage to the rights and interests of people. And these are seriously damaged by someone who departs from the norms of cognitive appropriateness, and this applies not only to other people but to the agent also. For in falling away from the principles of right reason into irrationality, one frustrates one's own *cognitive* objective of obliging answers to one's questions and getting at the truth of things.

After all, there are basically two sorts of reprehension, namely, reproach for folly and foolishness and reproach for wickedness and wrongdoing—that is to say, for mental and moral error. Sometimes, to be sure, the two are not totally disparate but interconnected. Someone who heedlessly exposes his actions and interactions to cognitive error—who is prepared to act in matters concerning others without getting the facts straight and thinking things out—is morally blameworthy thereby. Such a person is not just being foolish but merits moral reprehension as well, even in cases where no one is injured by his folly.

The lesson of these considerations is that moral and epistemic error are distinct sorts of things. Neither is moral error a cloaked version of cognitive error, nor is cognitive error itself automatically something in which a moral error is involved. Yet even if it is granted that the making and accepting of claims to objectively factual knowledge under the realistic conditions of cognitive fallibilism is not *immoral*, is there nevertheless not something *irrational* about it once the inherent defeasibility of such claims is recognized? If we recognize and admit that our acceptance-commitments "might be wrong" (even though we view this prospect as rather far-fetched), then why should we say that we *know* these things, thereby seemingly contradicting this realization? The answer is simply that this line of objection is based on a misleading premiss. The long and short of it is that our factual knowledge claims need not and should not be construed in so absolutistic a mode as to gainsay any and all possibility of error whatsoever—they should not be inflated beyond the range of reachability. Quite the reverse. Given the goals of the cognitive enterprise—achieving an intellectual and physical control over nature and commenting with one another effectively about this shared world—stating and accepting claims to objectively factual knowledge should and can be something altogether prudent, reasonable, and, above all, *justified*. Here, too, refraining from the risk of error is a policy that is self-defeating in the larger scheme of things.

SOME OBJECTIONS TO COGNITIVE PRUDENTIALISM

To be sure, someone might be tempted to object as follows: "Cognitive rationality is surely not primarily a matter of prudence, thus sidelining moral considerations. After all, man has a moral or quasimoral duty to make the most of his natural endowments. And making the most of our natural endowments calls for adherence to the rules of right reason. Accordingly, adherence to these rules becomes a matter of duty as well." This line of argumentation is mistaken, however. A circumstantially necessary prelude to the discharge of a moral duty does not itself thereby become a moral duty. (I may have a moral duty to honor my promise of being in a certain place at a certain time, and it might, in the circumstances, be a necessary condition thereof that I drive beyond the speed limit, but that does not make my driving beyond the speed limit itself a matter of moral duty.)

Again, somebody might object as follows: "Even if you are right in holding that what is at issue is a matter of the procedural principles of cognitive rationality, does this not still generate an ethical aspect through the higher-level principle that *People ought to be cognitively ra-*

tional?" The reply here is straightforward: Of course, people *ought* to be rational; this is something that one must admit and, indeed, insist upon. But this "ought" is not at bottom one of a specifically ethical or moral orientation. For people ought also to be perceptive, sensitive, intelligent, open-minded, healthy, handsome, and so on. Rather, the "ought" here is one of the cosmic fitness of things. It does not indicate an operative principle of human action but represents an idealized vision of the optimal arrangements of the world.[7] The world *ought* to be a place where things go properly. But in general people have no more a *duty* to be good believers than they have a *duty* to be good rememberers or good learners, however desirable it may be in the larger scheme of things for them to be so.[8] Yet is there not a moral duty to do all we can to realize the good, to enhance the ac-tualization of positive value in the world? Of course there is! But this holds for *every* sort of good or value. Our overt action in relation to all goods has an ethical dimension, but this does not establish these goods or values as specifically ethical ones. In sum, the epistemic ought is just not a moral ought: these two must be differentiated.

The individual who is defective in point of rationality—who rea-sons inadequately, thinks poorly, and argues badly—is akin to the person who is defective in point of intelligence. His failings are not *sins* but *defects,* not offenses but disabilities. They are more to be pit-ied than censured. (Of course, the case of *deliberate* transgression is something else again.) Insofar as reckless assertion beyond the avail-able evidence may, when given credence, predictively cause others to have and act on mistaken beliefs, it can also be wrongdoing. But this is a rather special case.

One key question of an "ethics of belief" is whether someone who stakes a claim to knowledge is, as the sceptic would have it, thereby automatically being hypocritical and involved in making an unwarranted and inappropriate assertion where "he actually does, or should, know better"? But this is surely not the case. The basic ground rules of language use have it that the way an assertion is standardly intended by its "sender" must be construed as correlative with the way it is to be construed by its "recipient." When I say, "I know that *p*," I must expect *you* to construe this circumstance as, "Rescher claims to know [or maintains he knows] that *p*." And if I am conscientiously concerned to preserve my credibility, I will only make such assertions in circumstances where I have good reason to believe them to be true. But their *actually* being true—as contradistinguished from my *holding* them to be true and having good (or excellent or effectively conclusive) grounds for this—is not and cannot be a legitimate precondition of my rational entitlement to make such an assertion. For the only handle that I have on the issue of the actual truth of *p* proceeds via the issue of whether there is, as best I can tell, good and sufficient reason for me to maintain *p*. To insist that the truth of *p* itself—independently of any justificatory warrant I may have to it—is a *precondition* of my rational entitlement to claim to know that *p* would be to impose an illegitimate (because *in principle* unrealizable) condition. For we have no *direct* access to the truth, independently of the warranting considerations that authorize our staking claims to its realization. It is one of the unfortunate but nevertheless inevitable aspects of our condition as finite knowers that we can and not infrequently will have rationally warranted belief in falsehoods. But there need be nothing reprehensible about it. We are, in this particular regard, more to be pitied than censured.

✕ 6 ✕
Error and Metaphysics

The very idea of error involves subscribing to some sort of realism: Error calls for incorrectness, for conflict with the actual facts, and were there no actual matter of fact there would be no error either. For error to be possible, there must be something distinctively objective and real to be wrong about. In a realm without any reality, a realm of mere appearances where all is illusion and delusion, no such thing as error is possible. One can be wrong only where there is something definite to be wrong about. The very idea of error commits us to a reality that differs from what it is thought to be and thereby requires a robust conception of reality. One's view of error is thus bound to align with one's theory of reality. For example, theoreticians who undifferentiatingly put being and nonbeing in the same box cannot possibly extract error from there. Thus the oriental mystic who denies reality altogether and sees everything mundane as an illusion is bound to error regarding the world as nonexistent or, if you prefer, all-pervasive—for lack of an authentic reality to contrast it with. And, again, error is equally unreal for the many-worlds theorist for whom all possibilities are just so many equivalent parts of one single all-encompassing manifold that accepts all possibilities as actual. ⟩

The doctrine of factual realism is a metaphysical position defined by the following contention: Being a fact does not depend on what people know/think/believe to be so; facts obtain objectively, independent of any and all such epistemic considerations. Such a doctrine immediately opens the door to what might be characterized as an error-based approach to metaphysical realism. The basic idea goes back to Plato's dialogue *Theaetetus*, where Socrates critiques the following idea: "False judgment [error] is the sort of misjudgment that occurs when a person confuses two things, both of which are distinct, through asserting that the one is the other by misidentifying something that really is with something else [that is not]" (*Theaetetus* 189 BC). The principal worry here centers on the problematic idea of a something that is not. But the issue has another, more metaphysical side as well. For obviously, if error arises from confusing what is with an unreal something else, the error could not be if "what actually is" were not acknowledged.

In one form or another this approach to realism has recurred in various guises over the years. Not only was it adumbrated in Plato's predecessors, but it rose to prominence once more in the thought of Josiah Royce, who in his 1885 classic *The Religious Aspect of Philosophy* made error the pivot-point of his deliberations. To begin with, he stressed the absolute inevitability of accepting the reality of error by reasoning essentially as follows: "Error is . . . defined as a judgment that does not agree with its object. In the erroneous judgment, subject and situation are so combined as, in the object, the corresponding elements are not included. And thus the judgment comes to be false. . . . But now consider our conviction that there is such a thing as error. Then either we are right, and then error exists, or we are wrong, and then error exists as well. Such a dilemma indicates the inevitability of error."[1]

The realization that we are sometimes mistaken is not a particularly edifying piece of knowledge. But it is at least something regarding which we cannot possibly be mistaken. So error, for Royce, is an "indubitable fact" on which realism can rely for a firm foundation.[2] For error to obtain—for a judgment to be untrue of the object—means that the object's actual condition is not as the judgment claims it to be, which, of course, requires an actual condition to realize this situation. So realism is home free. And not only is the concept of *error* inseparably linked to a commitment to realism, but this holds no less for the concept of *ignorance* as well. For if, as is surely often the case, we are (all of us!) ignorant of certain facts, then it must be that such facts, at least, obtain independently of what we think (be it individually or collectively).

In the end, a creature that concedes its susceptibility to error and ignorance has little choice but to acknowledge the contrast between what is and what is thought to be so—even though the creature can do this only in general terms, subject to an inescapable incapacity to provide concrete instances. Accordingly, a cognitive modesty that commits us to the recognition of potential error thereby also enjoins a commitment to realism in its wake. There is, overall, a powerful case to be made for factual realism from a basis of considerations regarding the limits of knowledge.[3] Clearly, whenever it can be established on the basis of general principles that there are certain matters of fact that we do not know or indeed even know of, then this too indicates the implausibility of holding that in regard to fact it is our thinking that makes it so. After all, when a question that must by its very nature actually be decided one way or the other is such that we ourselves cannot possibly decide it, then it becomes distinctly impracticable to ascribe the substance of that solution to us. But while this argumentation, too, is cogent, it represents an approach variant from that based on error. To argue for realism from error is to argue from a fault of commission. By contrast, to argue to this conclusion from ignorance is to argue from a fault of omission. So, while the up-shot is substantially the same, the route leading to this common de-struction is rather different. But either way, it transpires, somewhat ironically, that the ultimate basis of our commitment to realism does not lie in our cognitive power but in our cognitive debility—in the inexorable prospects of error and ignorance.

It is important to note, however, that the realism at issue with er-ror and ignorance is in both cases alike of a sort that does not take the categorical form: "Factual realism is correct since such-and-such is actually the case." Instead, it approaches the matter in a circuitously oblique manner. Its format is unabashedly: "If (as is indeed only too sensible) you are going to think that our cognitive situation is prob-lematically disadvantaged—not only open to ignorance or error but to some extent actually enmeshed in it—then you will have to en-dorse factual realism as well." Such argumentation clearly pivots not on what is but on what is thought to be—it looks at reality through the mediation of how we think of it.

It thus emerges as a key feature of a cognitively negative approach to factual realism that it illustrates the characteristic style of concep-tual idealism in that it really does not establish in a direct, ontologi-cal way that thought-independent reality exists. Instead, it takes the line of arguing that our conceptual scheme—and, in particular, our concept of error—is such that realism is inherently presupposed. In effect it argues that, "Given that we use the conception of error as we actually do, the very idea that error occurs demands (given the na-ture of the concept at issue) that we stand committed to the correla-tive existence of an objectively mind-independent reality." In sum, what such reasoning endeavors to establish is that the conceptual mechanisms in whose terms of reference our thought about these matters is formed stand committed to a thought-independent reality. But this affords no basis for any justified complaint. After all, as noted above, the request, "Don't tell me what you think to be so; just tell me what actually is independently of how you conceive of it" presents a challenge that, as a matter of principle, is impossible to meet. We have to be realistic (in the everyday sense of that term) about what sorts of expectations one can reasonably have and about what sorts of demands it is reasonable to make. To impose on cogent thought the real conditions and requisites whose realization is in principle impossible is decidedly inappropriate.

A WORLD IN ERROR? THE BUTTERFLY EFFECT

Consider the following hypothetical questions: If this world of ours indeed were created by a benign and omnipotent deity, would its patent defects show it to be an error? Is reality not simply one vast error? "Surely creating a better world would not be all that hard. After all, it would not have taken much to arrange some small accident that would have removed a Hitler or a Stalin from the scene. To figure out how this sort of thing could be arranged—to the world's vast improvement—is not rocket science!" Alas, dear objector, have you not ever heard of the butterfly effect? This phenomenon roots in the *sensitive dependence of outcomes on initial conditions* in chaos theory, where a tiny variation in the initial conditions of a dynamical system can issue in immense variations in the long-term behavior of the system. In short the butterfly effect sees the various aspects of reality as so interlaced in a web of rational interactions that changing anything, even if seemingly in minor ways, ultimately ramifies it into changing pretty much everything else.

Edward Norton Lorenz first analyzed the effect in a 1963 paper,[4] leading to the comment of one meteorologist that "if the theory were correct, one flap of a seagull's wings would be enough to alter the course of the weather forever.''[5] With this process, changing even one tiny aspect of nature—one single butterfly flutter—could have the most massive repercussions: tsunamis, droughts, ice ages; there is no limit. With this phenomenology in play, rewriting the course of the cosmos in the wake of even the smallest hypothetic change takes not just rocket science but something infinitely more.

The butterfly effect means that we can no longer be glib and facile about our ability to make improvements in the world by somehow removing this or that among its patent imperfections by well-intentioned readjustments. For what would need to be shown is that such a repair would not yield unintended and indeed altogether unforeseen consequences resulting in an overall inferior result. And this would be no easy task—and indeed could prove to be one far beyond our feeble powers. "But could this situation not have been avoided altogether? After all, that butterfly effect is the result of the situation that, in certain respects, the laws of nature have yielded a situation of the sort that mathematicians characterize as chaotic. Surely we could change the laws of nature to avoid this result." It is no doubt so. But now we have leapt from the frying pan into the fire. For in taking this line we propose to fiddle not merely with this or that specific occurrence in world history, but have toyed with the very laws of nature themselves. And this embarks us on the uncharted waters of a monumental second-order butterfly effect—one whose implications and ramifications are incalculable. The point is simple: The world's existing negativities taken in isolation are indeed remediable in theory. But to avert them in practice would require realizing an even larger array of negativities overall. The cost of avoiding those evils of this world would then be the realization of an even larger mass of misfortune.

But is it actually the case—really and truly—that the imperfect arrangements of this world nevertheless elevate it to a position of overall optimality? It would certainly take an intelligence far more powerful than mine—and perhaps even than *ours*—to establish so difficult and contentious a claim, something that would require distributive detail regarding an effectively unsurveyable manifold of items. It would clearly be an act of hubris to assert categorically one's ability to demonstrate in fact that the world's existence cannot be characterized as error. But what it does seem reasonable to assert is the merely *hypothetical* claim that if there is a satisfactory answer at all to the mistaken objective problem, then this affords a promising line of approach. Perhaps it is only just and proper that having set out from a question of a markedly hypothetical cast we should have to rest content with an answer whose status is comparably hypothetical.

This line of thought also opens the way to dealing with the theological problem of why a benevolent creator should produce a world that has such wide room for error. This so-called problem of error that greatly concerned seventeenth-century rationalist philosophers, such as Descartes, Spinoza, and Leibniz, is a cognitive version of the larger traditional problem of evil.[6] But the pursuit of this issue leads from philosophy into theology and thereby moves beyond the limits of our present concerns.

✕ 7 ✕
Historical Background

As viewed by Zeno of Elea and various ancient Greek thinkers who followed in his wake, cognitive error is something of a puzzle. For if, as they believed, meaningful thought and talk must appertain to what is and cannot deal in what is not, then error, being at variance with what is, becomes inaccessible to intelligible discourse, since it relates to a nonexistent what-is-not.

One promising way of addressing this puzzle was to say that while language at large deals with what indeed is, the specific instances of its application might become involved in a confusion in mistaking one perfectly real thing for another. So when a rose (which is actually red) is mistakenly said to be green, then we are not talking of a thing that is not (that is, some green rose) but rather are ascribing to a perfectly real object (the rose) a perfectly real property—although, in this instance, this particular pairing is inappropriate. This, in effect, was the position on the matter taken by Socrates in Plato's dialogues *Phaedo* and *Theaetetus*.

Specifically, in the *Theaetetus* Socrates pursues the question of how it is that if false judgment consists in thinking one thing to be another, such a thing is possible at all. Either both are clearly conceived, in which case we could not mistake one for another, or our conception of one of them is incomplete, unclear, and indistinct, in which case it is implausible that we should be prepared to regard it as identical with the other. For, as Socrates says (at 188B), it is surely implausible that someone should suppose that things he does not know actually are other things he does not know. Moreover, if thinking falsely were to think to be actually "the thing that is not," then to think what is not is to think nothing at all.[1] And such problematic conception of error would render its commission impracticable.

The problem that the platonic Socrates thus sought to resolve was part of the heritage of Parmenides and certain Sophists for whom it was implicit in the following apory: (1) People do occasionally err through accepting false statements. (2) False statements maintain that which is not. (3) There is no "that which is not": what is not does not exist; only what is exists. (4) Given (2) and (3), it follows that there just is no falsity—contrary to (1). Here, Plato has Socrates effectively rejecting premiss (2), holding, instead, that falsehood is not a matter of accord with a nonexistent irreality but rather one of mis-match with an existent reality. As against Parmenides and some of the Sophists, who went so far as to deny (1), such a view sensibly holds that error is not a matter of thinking about that which is not but rather of thinking of that which is differently from the way it is. Error accordingly does not engage nonbeing but rather being; it does not correspond positively to an inexistent irreality but rather corresponds negatively to an existent reality. On this basis, error is not a matching with the nonexistent but rather a mismatch among existents—as when the wrong bird has been snatched from an aviary (*Theaetetus* 199). It results when certain perfectly real features of perfectly real things are ascribed through some sort of mixup or confusion to yet another perfectly real thing where they just do not belong. Even our thought about intelligible forms can, as Plato sees it, go awry through mentally linking mutually incompatible items.

On such an approach to error, the whole business of a doctrine of nonbeing and irreality is something that an adequate account of error can simply bypass. As Plato himself puts it, the statement, "Theaetetus was sitting" will, when correct, "state about Theaetetus the things that are," while the statement that he is standing constitutes "a false statement that states about him things that are perfectly feasible and real in themselves, but simply different from the things that are [in the circumstances at hand]" and thereby claims, "things that are not as being so."[2]

From Plato's standpoint, the defect of the Eleatic position lay in his insistence that error had to have a correct (appropriately matched) characterization of the nonexistent nonfacts rather than an incorrect (inappropriately matched) characterization of the actual facts. For Parmenides nonbeing had (per impossible) to be for error to arise through concord, whereas as Plato saw it error arises through discord with the actualities. Here, Plato was surely right. It is not that false statements are true to the nonfacts, but simply that they are not true to the facts. Error is a matter not of the faithful representation of the nonfacts but rather of the unfaithful representation of the facts by claiming them to be different from what they are.

It might be complained that Plato's account provides no way to deal with statements about all-out nonexistents, such as flying saucers or the Easter rabbit, so that it would become impracticable to class as erroneous statements like, "There are flying saucers" or "The Easter rabbit exists." But this seems very problematic. Frisbees apart, saucer contraptions do not fly. Nor does the repertoire of rabbit activities include hiding colored eggs at Easter time. Discernible aspects of reality accordingly block the road to such contentions and qualify them as erroneous on exactly the sorts of grounds contemplated by and provided for in Plato's account of falsity and error.

As Plato already noted, a personal conviction of truth can prevail with equal force irrespective of whether its focus is something that is actually true or actually false.[3] No purely subjective criterion of error can be secure. In book 1 of Plato's *Republic*, Thrasymachus falls into difficulty because he refuses to acknowledge that a true ruler can commit error.[4] As ever, the exit from philosophical difficulty is through the doorway of distinctions. In *legal* matters the doctrine of sovereign immunity may indeed shield the ruler from error. But with *moral* considerations the matters is, of course, very different. Law is a manipulable artifact, but righteousness and justice are something else again.

LATER THINKERS

St. Thomas Aquinas distinguishes three major "defects of cognition," namely, unknowing or ignorance, error, and heresy (*nescientia vel ignorantia, error, et haeresis*). Error he characterizes as a matter of accepting the false in place of the true.[5] He goes on to observe that, "Error thus adds a certain [overt] act to mere ignorance, because one can be ignorant without passing judgment on the things one is ignorant of. One is then unknowing but not in error."

As Duns Scotus saw it, all error—cognitive and moral alike— stems from acts of will. Cognitive error arises from improper decisions to acceptance in matters of belief, and moral error arises from improper decisions to action in matters of practice. Responsibility for the occurrence of error is thus always grounded in man's free will—an element of that perversity characteristic of humans since the days of the Garden of Eden.

In his midfifteenth century books *De docta ignorantia* and *De conjec-*

tura, Nicholas of Cusa maintained that what we deem as knowledge is all conjecture and largely erroneous. Only through the divinely instituted capacity for our intuitive vision *(speculatio intuitiva)* of God himself—the sort of inspired apprehension at work in the experience of the mystics—does secure knowledge of actual truth become accessible to us frail mortals.

The ancient sceptics' insistence on the vulnerability of human judgment to error—and the generally pervasive rule of error in human affairs—constituted the focal point of Descartes' philosophy.[6] The rush to judgment before all the evidence is in is, for Descartes, an integral constituent of our human constitution and saddles the onus of error squarely on our backs.

Descartes inherited from the church fathers the big question of why error occurs at all in a world created by an intrinsically perfect divine designer. The answer he proposed had two parts: The first part is that error is unavoidable in a universe that contains us because intelligent beings must operate in the world under the aegis of general laws that reach beyond the limited scope of our restricted experience. The very laws that enable us to function must also operate under nonstandard circumstances that, being extraordinary, do not conform to the general run that is our guide. So, for example, the laws of optics that enable us to see do and must have it be that the straight stick held under water at an angle looks bent to us. The second part of his answer is that man comes to fall into error whenever he chooses, through his own free will, to give assent even when this is not objectively warranted. After all, the option of a suspension of belief is always open. Responsibility for error thus lies entirely in our own heedlessness.

Such a line of thought would seem to explain the occurrence of error in even a God-created universe. For while common experience teaches, so Descartes tells us, that we are subject to a veritable "infinity of errors,"[7] nevertheless, as he sees it the human intellect could not and would not of itself commit any errors without the acts of will represented by deliberated assent. So the responsibility for error lies entirely with us.[8] Error of omission is not a mere negative but a positive engagement with falsehood, an overtly willed commitment to a putative state of affairs that is not in fact actual.[9]

There are, to be sure, some difficulties here. The idea that error always arises from a fully voluntary decision can certainly be contested against Descartes, and against Scotus before him. Surely—so it can be objected—errors in belief and action can be engendered in such proceedings as indoctrination, brainwashing, subliminal suggestion, and the like.[10] However, when this sort of thing occurs, its source is still the freely deployed sinfulness and malignancy of man. It is just that the free will at work in such cases is not that of the victim of error but of the manipulator at work.

For Spinoza, error lies not so much in the perversity of human judgment (as with Descartes) but rather arises from misunderstanding. Moreover, "being ignorant and being in error are two different things," because the falsity at issue with error is not mere ignorance but "such a privation of knowledge as is involved, knowing that is inadequate, or in ideas that are inadequate or confused."[11] Error is not a mere blank in the canvas of knowledge but is filled in with what should not be there.

Leibniz characteristically rejected the Scotist-Cartesian view of error: "I do not admit that error depends on the will rather than the intellect. For to err is to believe to be true or false that which stands otherwise. . . . [Such misjudgment] does not depend on the will; it is a mis-judging rather than mis-willing."[12] As Leibniz saw it, the individual who errs is deluded rather than perverse and is more to be pitied than censured.

William James quite properly argued against W. K. Clifford that the enterprise of inquiry is governed not only by the negative injunction "Avoid error!" but no less importantly by the positive injunction "Achieve truth!" And, in the domain of objective fact—where the assertive *content* of our claims unavoidably outstrips information we can ever gather by way of supportive *evidence* for them—this goal of achieving truth inevitably demands (so James insisted) running a risk of error. There is nothing irrational, let alone *wrong*, about accepting this risk. Quite to the contrary, "a rule of thinking which would absolutely prevent me from acknowledging certain kinds of truth, if those kinds of truth were really there, would be an irrational rule."[13] Only by being willing to run in the cognitive race do we stand a chance, however slim, of winning it: "Nothing ventured, nothing gained." Running the risk of error is the most fundamental requisite of the cognitive life. As James cogently argued, if we want to engage in the cognitive enterprise—if we want to obtain answers to our questions about the world—we have no choice but to accept a risk of error, a risk that we cannot evade altogether, however ardently (and rightly!) we strive to reduce its magnitude.

The theme of error constituted a centerpiece in the philosophy of Josiah Royce, and the chapter "The Possibility of Error" was the fulcrum of the classic *The Religious Aspect of Philosophy*.[14] To Royce's mind, it is only through accepting the idea of Absolute Thought and Absolute Truth that we can get a proper conception of error as such. The very concept of error presupposes an absolute standard that it fails to reach. "What then is error? An error, we reply, is an incomplete thought, that to a higher thought, which included it and its intended object, is known as having failed."[15]

For F. H. Bradley, error and truth are not only coordinate but inextricably commingled. The difference is always one of degree: a matter of proportion rather than exclusive dichotomy: "There will be no truth which is entirely true, just as there will be no error which is totally false. With both alike, if taken strictly, it will be a question of amount, and will be a question of more or less. . . . truth and error, measured by the Absolute, must each be subject always to degrees."[16] Hyperbolic though this sounds, there is something to it.

In his *Some Main Problems of Philosophy*, G. E. Moore maintained that, "[cognitive] error always consists in believing some proposition which is false" and then explains falsity by maintaining that, "to say that belief is . . . false is to say that there is not in the universe any fact to which it corresponds."[17] Apart from overlooking errors of omission that arise from failures to recognize facts, this formulation involves other difficulties as well: The first part of Moore's contention is infelicitous and cumbersome. Propositions (about which Moore was in any case ambivalent) just need not be brought into it at all. One can simply say that a cognitive error consists in false belief (and could then go on to add that behavioral error is counterproductive action). The second part of Moore's contention is comparably infelicitous. Why, after all, bring being "in the universe" into it? Facts, after all, do not have *position* as things do or *location* as states of affairs do. (The dog is located in the room all right; the fact of its being yours is not.) Moreover, why not simply say that a false belief is one that conflicts with the actual facts? And why this business of *correspondence-to-the-universe*? Let it be that there are 5 people in the room. The arrangements of the universe certainly do not belie the totally nonerroneous belief that there are fewer than 578 people in the room. But do they *correspond* to it?

Then, too, there is the consideration that error can arise not only in relation to the *substance* of what is believed but also to its *grounds*. For even if what you accept is correct, you are nevertheless still in error when matters are seriously amiss with the grounds of your acceptance. Suppose someone thinks that 4 is a divisor of 98 and on the grounds of this belief thinks that 98 is not a prime number. This individual is still in error overall, the correctness of the belief that 98 is no prime notwithstanding, for while this belief is indeed true, it is, nevertheless, an erroneously held belief. Indeed, even a true belief that is inferred from true grounds is erroneously held if that inference is inappropriate. Thus if you think that $p \& q$ is always true when p is, and then on the basis of the truth of $2 \times 2 = 4$ infer that $2 \times 2 = 4 \& 4 \times 2 = 8$, and thereupon conclude that $4 \times 2 = 8$, your belief is still inappropriately and erroneously held, notwithstanding its patent truth. The point is that the phrase "error in belief" is equivocal between two senses, relating respectively to (1) the falsity of the belief itself, and (2) the incorrectness of the basis on which that belief is held. Here, as elsewhere, error can be a matter either of product or process—a circumstance that Moore's analysis of cognitive error simply ignored.

Bertrand Russell in his *Problems of Philosophy* adopted an equally inadequate view of error.[18] The belief that Desdemona loves Cassio is mistaken, so he holds, because the "complex unity" consisting of *Desdemona's love for Cassio* does not exist. However, this view of the matter is just plain weird. Is the belief "three is greater than five" false because of a nonexistent complex unity consisting of three's being greater than five? But what on earth sort of thing would such a complex unity be? Clearly, any such complex unity account of falsity manages to explain something that is fairly straightforward in terms of something that is profoundly obscure. So in the end Russell's analysis of error does not help us all that much. Error is not a matter of failing to conjure appropriately with complex sorts of abstract unities: it is just a matter of getting things wrong, of failing to capture the truth, as Plato had it.[19]

✕ 8 ✕
Error's Ramifications

Homo sapiens is a fallible creature of limited capacity, and error casts its shadow across the whole range of our affairs. In matters of agency we finite beings are limited not only in our ability to see how to make matters work out effectively for the realization of our ends but also in our ability to make appropriate judgments regarding the worth and value of those ends. And our moral nature is defective in motivation to act in the interests of the well being of the community at large. Moreover, error is the reverse side of the coin of knowledge. The prominence of error in our cognitive affairs is explained in part by the consideration that in resolving our questions there is generally only one way to get things right but a myriad of ways of getting them wrong. The risk, and, indeed, the reality, of error is an inherent feature of cognitive progress.

The pervasiveness of error in human affairs has substantial philosophical ramifications. The following principal categories are at issue here:

Philosophical anthropology: The inescapability of error joins our mortality in marking mankind as a limited and imperfect creature.

Epistemology: Error brings home to us the dualistic division between real and merely putative knowledge. For, unfortunately, we cannot in general see error as error; it does not bear its falsity on its sleeves. So we cannot identify truth with that which we accept as knowledge, the merely putative included. However, the progress of human knowledge is marked not only by the reduction of *ignorance* but the reduction of error as well.

Ontology: Error betokens the need to acknowledge the fallibilism of *Homo sapiens* as a creature of limited cognitive capacity. Its acknowledgment requires recognizing the possibility and frequent reality of getting things wrong. Accordingly, the very prospect of error precludes our identifying reality with that which we take to be real. The only realism we can sensibly endorse in relation to what we take ourselves to know is a realism of aspiration rather than realization.

Theology: While human weakness and incapacity, and thereby error, create *problems* from a theological point of view, a closer look at the issues shows that no insuperable *obstacles* are at issue here.

The circumstance that error has significant ramifications in each of these prime areas of philosophical concern establishes its prominence and importance in this field. But, overall, the most philosophically salient feature of error lies in its role as a characterizing hallmark of human finitude and imperfection. Notwithstanding its banality, the dictum "to err is human" is profound in its implications. And yet while acknowledging our condition as error-prone beings, we nonetheless do well not only to minimize the occurrence of error but also to mitigate its adverse consequences should it occur—as occur it will.

NOTES

CHAPTER 1: THE WAYS OF ERROR

1. See Gerson, "The Stoic Doctrine," in Stump et al., *Hamartia*, 1983, 119–47.

2. Royce, *The Religious Aspect of Philosophy* 1885/1930.

3. Collingwood, *Speculum Mentis*, 1924, 45–46.

4. Discussions of the topics sprang to life again in nineteenth-century Britain in the writings of Richard Whalely and especially J. S. Mill, who devoted bk. 5 of his *Logic* to the topic under the heading "Philosophy of Error."

5. See Hamblin, *Fallacies*, 1970. Note that theoretical fallacies (fallacies in formal reasoning) have been studied more extensively than *practical* fallacies (fallacies in matters of decision and action).

6. Compare Collingwood, *Speculum Mentis*, 1924, 295–96.

7. See Rescher, *Peirce's Philosophy of Science*, 1978.

8. See Mayo, *Error and the Growth of Experimental Knowledge*, 1996.

9. As a mathematical phatonist (I am, after all, a student of Alonzo Church's), I am prepared to accept numbers and other mathematical entities as authentic, identity-possessing (nonschematic) abstract items.

As such, they are not thought-artifacts—and, indeed, not created arti-facts of any sort. Their existence and nature is *sui generis,* and they stand outside the range of the present deliberations.

CHAPTER 2: THE DIALECTIC OF IGNORANCE AND ERROR

1. Arieti, "History, Hamartia, Herodotus," in Stump et al., *Hamartia,* 1983, 2–3.

2. But *important* for whom? For anyone who wants to understand the matter properly within the general domain of deliberation at issue. And this provides a basis for multiplying conceptions—for example, by distin-guishing between the *scientifically* important facts and those important in the context of *everyday life.* Think of Arthur Eddington's distinction between the scientists' table and the table of our ordinary experience. See Eddington, *The Nature of the Physical World*, 1929, ix–xi.

3. See Aquinas, *Summa theologica*, bk. 1, quest. 17, sec. 3.

4. Compare F. H. Bradley's thesis: "Error *is* truth, it is partial truth that is false only because partial and left incomplete." Bradley, *Appear-ance and Reality*, 1893, 169.

5. The paradox was formulated in Makinson, "The Paradox of the Preface," 1965, 205–207.

6. Your accepting them achieves more, but that's your doing, not mine.

7. It is thus perfectly possible for two people to communicate effec-tively about something that is wholly nonexistent and about which they have substantially discordant conceptions (for example, X's putative wife, where X is, in fact, unmarried, though one party is under the mis-impression that X is married to A, and the other under the misimpres-sion that X is married to B). The commonality of intent is the basis on which alone the exchange of information (or misinformation) and the discovery of error become possible. And this inheres, not in the actual arrangements of the world, but in our shared (conventionalized) inten-tion to talk about the same thing about X's wife or rather X's *putative* wife in the case at hand.

8. The justification of such imputations is treated more fully in ch. 9 of the author's *Induction*, 1980.

9. Spinoza, *Ethics,* bk. 1, axiom 6.

10. On these issues, see also the author's *Presumption*, 2006.

CHAPTER 3: SCEPTICISM AND THE RISK OF ERROR

1. Doyle, *The Sign of Four*, 1890, ch. 6.

2. For more detail about scepticism, see the author's *Scepticism*, 1980.

3. Aristotle, *Metaphysics*, IX, 10:1051b25. However, despite Aristotle's various sagacious observations regarding error, an actual *theory* of error cannot be credited to him. Compare Keeler, *The Problem of Error from Plato to Kant*, 1934, 40.

4. Fridtjof Nansen, as quoted in Huntford, *The Last Place on Earth*, 1985, 200.

CHAPTER 4: ERROR AND OVERSIMPLIFICATION

1. On this topic, see the author's *Scientific Progress*, 1978).

2. See B. W. Petley, *The Fundamental Physical Constants and the Frontiers of Measurement* (Bristol: Hilger, 1985).

3. On the structure of dialectical reasoning, see the author's *Dialectics* (Albany: State University of New York Press, 1977); and for the analogous role of such reasoning in philosophy, see *The Strife of Systems* (Pittsburgh, PA: University of Pittsburgh Press, 1985) and *Philosophical Dialectics* (Albany: State University of New York Press, 2006).

4. An interesting illustration of the extent to which lessons in the school of bitter experience have accustomed us to expect complexity is provided by the contrast between the pairs rudimentary/nuanced, unsophisticated/sophisticated, plain/elaborate, and simple/intricate. Note that in each case the second, complexity-reflective alternative has a distinctly more positive, or less negative, connotation than its opposite counterpart.

CHAPTER 5: ERROR AND MORALITY

1. A closer treatment of the legal dimension of error is found in Savigny's classic *System des Heutigen Römischen Rechts*, 1981.

2. See Apostle, "An Aristotelian Essay on Errors," in Stump et al., 1983, 97–117.

3. For example, in Janet Chance's ardent little book *Intellectual Crime*, 1933, one finds "the making of statements that outstrip the evidence" prominently enrolled on the register of this category of "crimes." See also Clifford, *Lectures and Essays*, 1886. In actual fact, Clifford did not adhere to this hyperbolic area of *scientific* knowledge; he took the line that man's scientific "knowledge" of nature rests on various principles that are not in the final analysis justified on cognitive grounds at all, but must be accounted for in terms of natural selection. The principle of uniformity of nature is a prime example, and "Nature is selecting for survival those individuals and races who act as if it were uniform; and hence the gradual spread of that belief over the civilized world." See *The Common Sense of the Exact Sciences* (London, 1885), 209.

4. See, for example, Chance, *Intellectual Crime*, 1933, 33–34. This tendency of thought is also found in John Locke. There is, he wrote, "one unerring mark by which a man may know whether he is a lover of truth for truth's sake," namely, *"the not entertaining of any proposition with greater assurance than the proofs it is built upon will warrant."* Quoted in Passmore, *A Hundred Years of Philosophy*, 1968, 95. Locke is sometimes cast in the role of the founder of the "ethics of belief." See, for example, Price, *Belief*, 1969, 130 ff., and compare note 3 above. But Locke hinges the matter wholly on what "the mind, if it will proceed rationally, ought to [do]." *Essay Concerning Human Understanding*, bk. IV, ch. 15. He sees the imperative at issue as strictly instrumental *vis-à-vis* rationality. Later on, however, the situation changes in this regard. Passmore speaks of the "striking degree of moral fervor" by which this precept was espoused by agnostic thinkers in nineteenth-century England.

5. James, *The Will to Believe and Other Essays in Popular Philosophy*, 1899, 27–28.

6. James wrote, *"We must know the truth* and *we must avoid error . . .* are two separable laws. . . . We may regard the chase for truth as paramount . . . or we may, on the other hand, treat the avoidance of error as more imperative, and let truth take its chance." *The Will to Believe and Other Essays in Popular Philosophy*, 17–18. The situation in ethics as between a negative morality ("Avoid evil!") and a positive morality ("Promote good!") is, of course, a parallel. For a useful outline of the James-Clifford controversy and its background, see Kauber, "The Foundations of James' Ethics of Belief," 1974, where the relevant issues are set out and further references to the literature given. See also Kauber's, "Does James' Ethics of Belief Rest on a Mistake?" 1974. For a particularly interesting recent treatment, see Roderick Chisholm, "Lewis' Ethics of Belief," 1968, 223 ff.; compare Firth, "Chisholm and the Ethics of Belief," 1959, 493–506. See also Hare and Madden, "William James, Dickinson Miller, and C. J. Ducasse on the Ethics of Belief," *Transactions of the Charles S. Peirce Society,* 1969; and Williams, "Deciding to Believe," 1970, 95. More recently, see Hare and Kauber, "The Right and Duty to Will to Believe," 1974; Muyskens, "James' Defense of a Believing Attitude in Religion," 1974; and Johanson, "The 'Will to Believe' and the Ethics of Belief," 1975. For various ramifications of the James-Clifford controversy regarding the ethics of belief, see the interesting essay by Michalos, "The Morality of Cognitive Decision Making," 1976.

7. Of course, whenever such an "ought" of cosmic fitness is operative, there is a correlative duty to cultivate and promote its realization. But this represents quite a different issue. People ought to speak correctly or do their sums properly, but that does not make departures from correct speech or correct arithmetic into *ethical* transgressions.

8. The "ought" at issue is what I have elsewhere called that of *evaluative metaphysics,* in contrast with that of *normative ethics*—it is, if you like, the moral ought of a world creator rather than of a world occupant. See "The Dimensions of Metaphysics," in the author's *Essays in Philosophical Analysis* (Pittsburgh, PA: University of Pittsburgh Press, 1969), 229–54, where the relationship between these two modes of deontology is explored.

CHAPTER 6: ERROR AND METAPHYSICS

1. Royce, *The Religious Aspect of Philosophy*, 1885, ch. 11, especially pp. 396–97.

2. See James Courant in R. A. Putnam, *The Cambridge Companion to William James*, 1997, 187–89.

3. See the author's *Empirical Inquiry*, 1980; *Realistic Pragmatism*, 2000; and *Realism and Pragmatic Epistemology*, 2005. See also Vollmer, *Wissenschaftstheorie am Einsatz*, 1993.

4. Lorenz, "Deterministic Nonperiodic Flow," 1963.

5. Lorenz's discussion gave rise to New Line Cinema's 2004 feature film *The Butterfly Effect* starring Ashton Kutcher and Amy Smart.

6. On the theory of error of these three thinkers see, respectively, the essays by Belaval, Curley, and Maitra cited in the bibliography.

CHAPTER 7: HISTORICAL BACKGROUND

1. Plato, *Theaetetus*, 189b.

2. See *Sophist* 263b, and *Theaetetus* 192c.

3. On Plato's theory of error, see Levi, "La teoria stocia della verità e dell'errore," 1928.

4. Plato, *Republic*, 340d–e.

5. "Error vero supra ignorantiam addit applicationem mentis ad contrarium veritatis, ad errorem enim pertinet approbare falsis pro veris." Aquinas, *De malo*, quest. 3, art. 7.

6. The *locus classicus* here is bk. 2 of Descartes' *Meditations on First Philosophy*.

7. Descartes, *Meditations*, bk. 4, sec. 3.

8. Regarding Descartes on error, see Wilson, *Descartes*, 1978, as well as the essays by Belaval and Caton cited in the bibliography.

9. This simple idea is elaborately argued in Brochard, *De l'erreur*, 1897.

10. This point is argued by Thalberg in "Error," 1967.

11. Spinoza, *Ethics*, bk. 2, prop. 35.

12. Leibniz, "Cartesian Animadversiones," 1885.

13. James, *The Will to Believe and Other Essays in Popular Philosophy*, 1899.

14. Royce, *The Religious Aspect of Philosophy*, 1887.

15. Royce, *The Religious Aspect of Philosophy*, 1887, 431.

16. Bradley, *Appearance and Reality*, 1879, 362. Compare Joachim, *The Nature of Truth*, 1906), 118–19.

17. Moore, *Some Main Problems of Philosophy*, 1953, 66, 277.

18. Russell, *Problems of Philosophy*, 1959.

19. A good deal of historical information on error and its philosophical ramifications is contained in Schwarz, *Der Irrtum in der Philosophie*, 1934.

BIBLIOGRAPHY

Apostle, Hippocrates G., "An Aristotelian Essay on Error," in Stump et al. 1983, 97–117.

Aquinas, Thomas, *De malo*.

———, *Summa theologica*.

Arieti, James A., "History, Hamartia, Herodotus," in Stump et al. 1983, 1–25.

Aristotle, *Metaphysics*.

Augustine, *Contra Mendacium*.

———, *De Mendacio*.

Baldner, Steven, "The Use of Scripture for the Refutation of Error According to St. Thomas Aquinas," in Stump et al. 1983, 149–69.

Belaval, Yves, "Le probleme de l'erreur chez Leibniz," *Zeitschrift für Philosophische Forschung* 20 (1966): 381–95.

Bradley, F. H., *Appearance and Reality* (Oxford: Clarendon Press, 1893).

Brochard, Victor, *De l'erreur,* 5th ed. (Paris: Alcan, 1997).

Caton, Hiram, "Will and Reason in Descartes' Theory of Error," *Journal of Philosophy* 72 (1975): 87–104.

Cartwright, Nancy, *How the Laws of Physics Lie* (Oxford: Clarendon Press, 1983).

Chance, Janet, *Intellectual Crime* (London: N. Douglas, 1933).

Chisholm, Roderick, "Lewis' Ethics of Belief," in *The Philosophy of C. I. Lewis,* ed. P. A. Schilpp (La Salle, 1968).

Clifford, W. K., *Lectures and Essays*, 2nd ed., ed. L. Stephen and F. Pollock (London: Macmillan, 1886); originally published in *Contemporary Review* 30 (1877): 42–54.

———, *The Common Sense of the Exact Sciences* (London: Macmillan, 1885).

Collingwood, R. G., *Speculum Mentis or the Map of Knowledge* (Oxford: Clarendon Press, 1924).

Curley, E. M., "Descartes, Spinoza, and the Ethics of Belief," in *Spinoza: Essays in Interpretation*, ed. E. Freeman and M. Mandelbaum (LaSalle, IL: Open Court, 1975).

Descartes, René, *The Principles of Philosophy*.

———, *Meditations on First Philosophy*.

Doyle, Arthur Conan, *The Sign of Four* (1890).

Eddington, Arthur S., *The Nature of the Physical World* (Cambridge: Cambridge University Press, 1929).

Evans, J. L., "Error and the Will," *Philosophy* 38 (1963): 136–48.

Fecher, Vincent John, *Error, Deception, and Incomplete Truth* (Rome: Catholic Book Agency, 1975).

Firth, Roderick, "Chisholm and the Ethics of Belief," *The Philosophical Review* 68 (1959): 493–506.

Fisher, R. A., "Statistical Methods and Scientific Induction," *Journal of the Royal Statistical Society* 17 (1955): 69–78.

Gerson, Lloyd, "The Stoic Doctrine: All Errors Are Equal,'" in Stump et al. 1983, 119–47.

Hacking, Ian, *Logic of Statistical Inference* (Cambridge: Cambridge University Press, 1965).

Hamblin, Charles, *Fallacies* (London: Methuen, 1970).

Hare, Peter, and Peter Kauber, "The Right and Duty to Will to Believe," *Canadian Journal of Philosophy* 4 (1974): 327–43.

Hare, Peter, and Edward Madden, "William James, Dickinson Miller, and C. J. Ducasse on the Ethics of Belief," *Transactions of the Charles S. Peirce Society* 5 (Autumn 1969): 115–29.

Huntford, Richard, *The Last Place on Earth* (New York: Atheneum, 1985).

James, William, *The Will to Believe and Other Essays in Popular Philosophy* (New York: Longmans, 1899).

Jeffrey, Richard, *The Logic of Decision* (Chicago, IL: University of Chicago Press, 1965).

Joachim, H. H., *The Nature of the Truth* (Oxford: Clarendon Press, 1906).

Johanson. A. E., "'The Will to Believe' and the Ethics of Belief," *Transactions of the Charles S. Peirce Society* 11 (Spring 1975): 110–27.

Joseph, H. W. B., *An Introduction to Logic* (Oxford: Clarendon Press, 1906).

Kalechofsky, Robert, *The Persistence of Error* (Lanham, MD: University Press of America, 1982).

Kauber, Peter, "The Foundations of James' Ethics of Belief," *Ethics* 84 (1974): 151–66.

———, "Does James' Ethics of Belief Rest on a Mistake?" *Southern Journal of Philosophy* 12 (1974): 201–14.

———, "The Right and Duty to Will to Believe," *Canadian Journal of Philosophy* 4 (December 1974): 327–43.

Keeler, Leo, "Aristotle on the Problem of Error," *Gregorianum* 13 (1932): 241–60.

———, *The Problem of Error from Plato to Kant* (Rome: Apud Aedes Universitatis Gregorianae, 1934).

Kuhn, Thomas, *The Structure of Scientific Revolutions* (Chicago, IL: University of Chicago Press, 1962).

Lakatos, Imre, and Alan Musgrave, eds., *Criticism and the Growth of Knowledge* (Cambridge: Cambridge University Press, 1970).

Lebacqz, Joseph, "What Is Error?" *Heythrop Journal* 6 (1925): 171–88.

Leibniz, Gottfried Wilhelm, "Cartesian Animadversions," in *Philosophische Schriften,* vol. 6, ed. C. I. Gerhardt (Berlin: Weidmann, 1885).

Lenz, J. W., "Induction as Self-Corrective," *Studies in the Philosophy of Charles Sanders Peirce* (Amherst: University of Massachusetts Press, 1964).

Levi, Adolfo, "Il problema dell'erronre nella filosofia greca prioma di Platone," *Revue d'Historie de la Philosophie* 4 (1930): 115–28.

———, *Il problema dell'errore nella metafisica e nella gnoseologia di Plantone* (Padova: Liviana Editrice, 1970).

———, "La teoria stocia della verità e dell'errore" *Reve d'Histoire de la Philosophie* 2 (1928): 113–32.

———, "Il problema dell'errore nell'epicureismo," *Revista Critica di Storia della Filosophia* 5 (1950): 50–44.

———, "Il problema dell'errore nello scetticismo antico," *Revista di Filosofia* 40 (1949): 273–87.

———, "Il problema dell'errore in Filone d'Alessandria," *Rivista Critica di Storia della Filosofia* 5 (1950): 281–94.

———, "Il concetto dell'errore nella filosofia di Plotino," *Filosofia* 2 (1951): 213–28.

———, "Il problema dell'errore nella filosofia di B. Spinoza," *Sophia* (Palermo) 1 (1933): 144–58.

———, "Il problema dell'errore nella filosofia di Leibniz," *Rndiconti del R. Istituto Lombardo di Scienze e Lettere, Adunanza 7 Marzo 1929*, series 2, vol. 72, fasc. vi–x, 207–19.

———, "Il problema dell'errore nella filosofia di Resmini," *Revista de Filosofia* 16 (1925): 315–44.

Levi, Isaac, "On the Seriousness of Mistakes," in *Decisions and Revisions: Philosophical Essays on Knowledge and Value*, 14–33. First published in *Philosophy of Science* 29 (1962): 47–65.

Levin, Michael E., "On Theory Change and Meaning Change," *Philosophy of Science* 46 (1979): 407–24.

Locke, John, *Essays Concerning Human Understanding*.

Madden, Edward, "William James, Dickinson Miller, and C. J. Ducasse on the Ethics of Belief," *Transactions of the Charles S. Peirce Society* 5 (Autumn 1969): 115–29.

Mahler, Karl, *Die Entstehung des Irrtums bei Descartes und bei Spinoza* (Leipzig: Heller, 1910).

Maitra, Keya, "Leibniz's Account of Error," *International Journal of Philosophical Studies* 10 (2002): 63–73.

Makinson, D. C., "The Paradox of the Preface," *Analysis* 25 (1965): 205–7.

Mayo, Deborah G., *Error and the Growth of Experimental Knowledge* (Chicago, IL: University of Chicago Press, 1996).

Michalos, Alex C., "The Morality of Cognitive Decision Making," in *Action Theory*, ed. M. Brand and D. Walton (Dordrecht: D. Reidel, 1976).

Mill. J. S., *Logic*.

Moore, G. E., *Some Main Problems of Philosophy* (London: Allen & Unwin; New York: Humanities Press, 1953).

Muyskens, James, "James' Defense of a Believing Attitude in Religion," *Transactions of the Charles S. Peirce Society* 10 (Winter 1974): 44–54.

Nicolas, Jean-Hervé, "Le problème de l'erreur," *Revue Thomiste* 52 (1952): 328–57, 528–66.

Nugent, James Brennan, "Error," *New Catholic Encyclopedia*, vol. 5 (1967), 521.

O'Farrell, Francis Philip, "Falsity," *New Catholic Encyclopedia*, vol. 5 (1967), 824–25.

Passmore, John, *A Hundred Years of Philosophy* (Harmondsworth: Penguin Books, 1968).

Plato, *The Republic*.

———, *The Sophist*.

———, *Theaetetus*.

Popper, Karl, *The Logic of Scientific Discovery* (New York: Basic Books, 1959).

———, *Conjectures and Refutations: The Growth of Scientific Knowledge* (New York: Basic Books, 1962).

———, *Objective Knowledge: An Evolutionary Approach* (Oxford: Oxford University Press, 1979).

Price, H. H., *Belief* (London: Macmillan, 1969).

Prussen, Jules, "De l'erreur," *Revue de Métaphysique et de Morale* 66 (1961): 116–35.

Putnam, Ruth Anna, ed., *The Cambridge Companion to William James* (Cambridge: Cambridge University Press, 1997).

Radnitzky, G. and G. Andersson, eds., "Progress and Rationality in Science," *Boston Studies in the Philosophy of Science* 58 (1978): 162–79.

Rescher, Nicholas, *Peirce's Philosophy of Science: Critical Studies in His Theory of Induction and Scientific Method* (Notre Dame, IN: University of Notre Dame Press, 1978).

———, *Empirical Inquiry* (Totowa, NJ: Rowman & Littlefield, 1980).

———, *Induction* (Oxford: Basil Blackwell, 1980).

———, *Scepticism* (Oxford: Basil Blackwell, 1980).

———, *Realistic Pragmatism* (Albany: State University of New York Press, 2000).

———, *Realism and Pragmatic Epistemology* (Pittsburgh, PA: University of Pittsburgh Press, 2005).

Roland-Gosselin, M-D., "La théorie thomiste de l'erreur," *Mélanges Thomistes Publiés à l'occasion du Vie Cenenaire de la Canonisation de St. Thomas d'Aquin*, "Bibliothéque Thomiste," vol. 3 (1923), 253–74.

Rosenthal, David, "Will and the Theory of Judgment," in *Essays on Descartes' Meditations*, ed. A. O. Rorty (Berkeley: University of California Press, 1986).

Royce, Josiah, *The Religious Aspect of Philosophy: A Critique of the Basis of Conduct and of Faith*, 2nd ed. (London: Methuen, 1885/1930).

Russell, Bertrand, *Human Knowledge, Its Scope and Limits* (London: Allen and Unwin, 1966; first published in 1948).

———, *Problems of Philosophy* (New York: Oxford University Press, 1959).

Salmon, Wesley, *The Foundations of Scientific Inference* (Pittsburgh, PA: University of Pittsburgh Press, 1966).

Savage, L. J., *Statistics: Uncertainty and Behavior* (New York: Houghton Mifflin, 1968).

von Savigny, F. K., *System des Heutigen Römischen Rechts* (Aalen: Scientian Verlag, 1981).

Schwab, Friedrich, *De fontibus errorum* (Heidelberg, 1769).

Schwarz, Baldwin, *Der Irrtum in der Philosophie* (Münster: Aschendorff, 1934).

Spinoza, Benedictus de, *Ethics*.

Stump, Donald V., James A. Arieti, Lloyd Gerson, and Eleanor Stump, eds., *Hamartia: The Concept of Error in the Western Tradition* (New York: Edwin Mellen Press, 1983).

Thalberg, Irving, "Error," *The Encyclopedia of Philosophy*, vol. 3, ed. Paul Edwards (New York: Macmillen, 1967), 45–48.

Thomas, James, "Maritain's Criticism of Descartes' Theory of Error," *Maritain Studies* 15 (1999): 108–19.

Viglino, Ugo, "Errore," *Encyclopedia Cattolica*, vol. 5 (Vatican City: Ente per l'Enciclopedia Cattolica e per il Libra Cattolica, 1950), 519–22.

Vollmer, Gerhard, *Wissenschaftstheorie am Einsatz* (Stuttgart: Hirzel, 1993).

Walsh, Francis, "Error in the Making," *New Scholasticism* 2 (1928): 103–14.

Williams, Bernard, "Deciding to Believe," *Language, Belief, and Metaphysics,* ed. Howard Kiefer and Milton Munitz (Albany: State University of New York Press, 1970).

———, *Descartes: The Project of Pure Inquiry* (London: Penguin, 1978).

Wilson, Margaret D., *Descartes* (New York: Routledge 1978).

INDEX OF NAMES